THE SEGREGATED INFORMATION HIGHWAY

Information Literacy in Higher Education

YUSUF SAYED

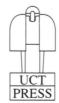

University of Cape Town Press
Calico / Infolit

University of Cape Town Press (Pty) Ltd
University of Cape Town
Private Bag, Rondebosch
7701 Cape Town
South Africa

and

Infolit Project, Adamastor Trust
14 Greenwich Grove
Station Road, Rondebosch
7000 Cape Town
South Africa

First published 1998

ISBN: 1-919713-05-0

Cover design: Jos Thorne
Set in 10 pt Sabon by RHT desktop publishing cc, Durbanville
Printed and bound by Rustica Press, Cape Town

Contents

List of Abbreviations

CAD	Computer-Aided Design
Calico	Cape Library Co-operative
CD-ROM	Compact-Disk Read Only Memory
CHAID	Chi-Squared Automatic Interaction Detection
CT	Cape Technikon
HAI	Historically advantaged institutions
HDI	Historically disadvantaged institutions
Infolit	Information-Literacy Project
IT	Information technology
PT	Peninsula Technikon
SPSS	Statistical Package for Social Sciences
UCT	University of Cape Town
US	University of Stellenbosch
UWC	University of the Western Cape
WCTIT	Western Cape Tertiary Institutions Trust
WGLIT	Working Group on Libraries and Information Technologies

List of Tables

List of Graphs

List of Charts

Foreword

It is easy (and entirely wrong) to dismiss the handling of information as being at the first level of educational development: being informed, or knowing how to become informed about a topic or discipline, is far from really understanding that topic or discipline or being able to use it at a high level in creative and productive ways.

Yet information literacy *is* a higher-order state of educational development, and it *does* have a great deal to do with understanding and mastery of a topic or discipline. This is because items of information vary in their value, validity and weight, and especially in their functionality as intellectual and practical tools. Knowing that a particular library in your immediate vicinity has an encyclopaedia (published in 1996) in which many details are provided of a thousand of the world's major business schools is a more helpful piece of information than a flier retrieved from your postbox informing you that you can study business management by correspondence with the Larry Flynt School of Business in Mobile, Alabama. Alternatively, knowing that the recommended references at the end of textbook chapters are unlikely to be as up to date as the references in current reviews in core journals is a higher-order item of information that provides a powerful lever for access to relevant further information.

Information literacy is thus a "key skill" similar to other foundation skills such as mathematics, statistics, language and communication. The electronic world-brain of the twenty-first century will make information discrimination and handling skills more and more valuable.

The Infolit Project is an ambitious attempt to ensure that the five tertiary institutions in the Western Cape are equipped maximally to develop the key skill of information literacy in every student and member of staff. A Needs Analysis is a necessary start of such an enterprise. The Adamastor Trust (Western Cape Tertiary Institutions Trust) is grateful to the author of this study, to the Reader's Digest Association for generous sponsorship, and to the Council of Library Directors for its support and encouragement. We look forward to significant results in the future.

Professor Wieland Gevers
Chair: Adamastor Trust
January 1998

Preface

Over the past decade, global developments and the reconstruction of South African society have heralded opportunities for fundamentally improving the quality of education. Extensive South African investigations such as that of the National Commission on Higher Education have identified the need for transformation of the education sector premised upon two sets of factors, "firstly, the profound deficiencies of the present system which inhibit its ability to meet the moral, social and economic demands of the new South Africa; and, secondly, a context of unprecedented national and global opportunities and challenges" (Department of Education 1996: 1).

The challenges to provide quality education in the context of increasing demand and to redress historical imbalances continue to occupy the minds of many educationalists. Central to these discussions is a concern not only with providing greater access to education, but with ensuring learners' capacity to participate fully in the educational system. This capacity is integrally linked to a range of literacies including the ability to learn and to use information critically. The shift away from rote-learning towards student-centered, life-long learning, from consumerism to active participation has forced the issue of information literacy onto the educational agenda.

In undertaking the mission to advance information literacy for purposes of promoting quality education, Infolit identified the need to comprehend levels of information literacy among its primary constituents. This study is the initial step in a process of developing a coherent policy framework for the advancement of information-literacy education in the Western Cape region. It serves to provide strategic direction for consideration by various players, including educational managers, academic planners and developers, academics, teachers and librarians. The study acknowledges areas in need of further investigation, but nonetheless offers a platform for further discussion and consideration.

A study of this nature would not have been made possible without the active support and participation of the Research Resource Group. The group comprised academics from the five institutions in the region: Hilton Fransman, Johann Mouton, Mary Nassimbeni, Philip Parsons and Yusuf Sayed. They provided invaluable research support from the design of the research project to the production of this book and acted as liaison persons at the five institutions. I appreciate the considerable time and effort they invested in the project, auguring well for future collaborative research. I would also like to thank Karin de Jager and Yusuf Sayed for carrying out the research. In particular, I would like to express my gratitude to Yusuf Sayed for his work as the project leader and for producing the final book with a contribution by Karin de Jager.

Cathy-Mae Karelse
Infolit Director

Acknowledgements

The Needs-Assessment Study was made possible by the support of numerous people. As director of Infolit I would like to extend my personal thanks to them all for their invaluable assistance and critical commentary. In particular, the following deserve a special vote of thanks:

- Reader's Digest whose generous support of the Infolit project made this study possible
- The Infolit Steering Committee for their active endorsement of the study
- The Adamastor Trust for their support and assistance in facilitating the study
- The Resource Group, Dr Hilton Fransman, Professor Johann Mouton, Dr Mary Nassimbeni, Professor Phillip Parsons and Dr Yusuf Sayed, for their critical advice and support
- Professor Johann Mouton provided an invaluable service in assisting with the analysis of the data and generating the tables upon which this report is based.
- Dr Karin de Jager as Senior Researcher provided valuable and critical research work; her contribution to the research process was enormously beneficial; she was specifically responsible for producing Chapter 4 of this report
- Ms Kate Whittaker as Research Administrator shouldered the responsibility for facilitating the research at an administrative level; she showed total dedication to the task
- The fieldworkers and lead co-ordinators for their resilience and resourcefulness in administering the questionnaires at the various institutions
- The students and staff at the five institutions for their time in completing the questionnaire and attending the interviews; without their active participation this book would not have been possible
- The various personnel involved in the Calico Van Service for their assistance in the distribution of the questionnaires.

Cathy-Mae Karelse
Infolit Director

Knowledge is of two kinds: we know a subject ourselves,
or we know where we can find information upon it.
Samuel Johnson 1791

Introduction

Motivation for the study

Information-society development has generated transformation at all levels in society. Within the context of globalisation, education and library sectors have been foci of change. In the South African context, concerns with restructuring an education system which enhances learning while balancing challenges of globalisation with those of corrective measures to redress imbalances, has led in part to collaborative ventures. One such co-operative is the Western Cape Tertiary Institutions Trust[1] which aims to promote co-operation among higher-education institutions in the Western Cape region. One of its co-operative projects, Calico (the Cape Library Co-operative), a consortium of the five higher-education institutional libraries, was established to provide a single seamless library and information system to the students and staff at these institutions.

In recognising the need to enhance teaching and learning throughout the region, Calico stated that one of its aims is "to promote information literacy ... to improve quality of life and economic well-being". This vision resulted in a project proposal to form Infolit, an information-literacy project with a five-year development programme. The programme identified the need to develop innovative pilot projects which would promote information literacy and develop successful models which could be spread across the region. In combination with this strategy, an important component of Infolit's brief was to investigate the state of information literacy across the five institutions with a view to understanding levels of information literacy and related needs as well as gaps in information provision.

These facets of Infolit's programme led to the formulation of a Needs-Assessment Study proposal. The study set out to investigate the state of information literacy at the five higher-education institutions. It was designed to identify appropriate interventions which would enhance levels of information literacy among learners in the region, by assessing their information-literacy abilities and needs. Following Infolit's formation in late 1995, the Needs-Assessment Study commenced in early 1996.

Aims and objectives of the study

The investigation aimed to provide:

- a systematic profile of information literacy which would be of assistance to the five institutions in responding to global information changes;
- an audit of students' information-literacy abilities and needs across the five institutions in the Western Cape regarding the specific needs and competencies they felt should be included in existing programmes as well as their information-literacy needs;
- comparative examples of information-literacy programmes in other countries with special reference to institutional policies and implementation strategies;
- key areas for strategic intervention based on the analysis of information literacy in the region.

Overview of the book

This book outlines the process and results of the Needs-Assessment Study and consists of eight chapters. The first chapter discusses understandings of the concept of information literacy based upon a review of the literature and discussions with key informants. It specifically outlines the definition of information literacy used for the study. Chapter 2 contextualises information literacy in the local and global contexts. Chapter 3 outlines the methodology of the study, while Chapter 4 provides a global overview of the state of information literacy at the five institutions in the region. Chapter 5 discusses students' information-literacy abilities and needs based on identified indices. Chapter 6 analyses the key predictor variables which explain the pattern of information-literacy abilities and needs that emerge from responses to the questionnaire. Chapter 7 provides a synopsis of the findings, and provides key recommendations for future information-literacy work. The conclusion of the book (Chapter 8) presents future directions for the Infolit project.

Note

[1] During the production of this book, WCTIT was renamed the Adamastor Trust.

1

The Concept of Information Literacy

The literature on information literacy, particularly with a focus on higher education, has recently been particularly evident (see Rader 1994). This increase in literature attests to the changing nature of information in our society and the move towards the information society. Information literacy has thus become a growing field of academic inquiry and research.

This chapter reviews mainly the literature published during the period 1993 to 1995. However, the present chapter does not presume to review exhaustively all articles published during this period. Instead, key texts which signify general trends and highlight important issues related to the notion of information literacy are identified and discussed.

As part of the process of generating a South African-specific definition of information literacy, it was decided to conduct a series of focus-group interviews with key strategic informants who have both experience and understanding of the field. Ultimately, the aim was to arrive at a common understanding and definition of information literacy on which to base and develop the research instruments. At the same time, a survey of recent literature was launched.

Reviewing definitions

The notion of information literacy emerged in the 1970s spurred on by the advent of new information technologies, and consequently signalled the need for libraries and librarians to redefine their roles in this context. The definitions of information literacy proposed in the literature reviewed can be situated on a continuum ranging from those which are narrow and specific to the more global and encompassing ones. Narrow and specific definitions emphasise mainly skills necessary to handle new forms of information technology and conceive of information literacy as mastery and understanding of technologies that transmit and offer information. An example of this approach would be definitions which mainly or solely focus on "narrow skilling", in particular on computer literacy, which is perceived to be necessary for handling new forms of information technology. Global definitions emphasise access to sources of information, skills to locate information and critical evaluation of information. The following lengthy exposition of the abilities to be acquired by the information literate (by Bruce (1995: 163) provides a representative example of such definitions:

> *"... people ... should ... be able to master the skills of managing and using information generated through new information technologies."*

understanding the nature of the information society; acquiring values that promote information access and use

- being able to implement the processes of identifying an information need
- locating, retrieving, evaluating and synthesising the information required
- developing a high level of communication skills, including the ability to communicate with colleagues and information professionals
- developing a sound knowledge of information sources, including network sources, and strategies for using them
- developing the ability to manage the information retrieved through the appropriate use of, for example, word-processors and bibliographic management software
- developing a familiarity with the hardware of information technology, books, newspapers, videos, compact disks, computers and all their accompanying apparatus.

Using the above global definition, the various sub-concepts that develop out of the concept of information literacy, will be analysed.

Information literacy and basic literacy

Most definitions of information literacy suggest that it is a literacy akin to reading and writing. Thus, just as much as people are able to read and write, they should also be able to master the skills of managing and using information generated through new information technologies. Information literacy is therefore part of other literacies and some are dependent on others such as reading and writing. This idea is clearly expressed by Makhubela and Koen (1995: 14), who state that "... information literacy contributes to a higher level of literacy!" Thus, information literacy presupposes the possession of basic reading, writing and numeracy skills, and contributes and advances on these literacies in the information age. In the South African higher-education context, however, the acquisition of this skill must go hand in hand with mastering "academic literacy". Karelse and Underwood (1996) argue further that information literacy is not simply a number of skills hierarchically linked. Instead, they suggest that information literacy refers to an approach to teaching and learning which enables citizens to muster the appropriate techniques to solve a problem.

Information literacy and location skills

All definitions of information literacy emphasise the fact that for people to be information-literate, they should be able to locate the sources of information. This requires the skills of knowing how to access various information sources and includes such skills as the ability to utilise a library, a computer and the Internet. These skills require a high degree of exposure to, and familiarity with, the various sources of information. McClure (1994) refers to these skills as network literacy, traditional literacy, media literacy and computer literacy. Thus, location skills refer to the ensemble of abilities and skills that allows an individual to identify and find sources of information.

"... the notion of information literacy implies that once the information is sourced, an individual should be able to both critically evaluate and use such information to solve a particular problem or task."

Information literacy and critical-thinking skills

The ability to access and manipulate information from various sources is a necessary but not sufficient condition for definitions of information literacy. All definitions argue that the notion of information literacy implies that once the information is sourced, an individual should be able to both critically evaluate and use such information to solve a particular problem or task. Some definitions (McClure 1994, for example) go as far as to suggest that all information-literacy activities are directed towards solving problems. This definition is too limiting, since all instances of information-searching are not solely directed towards an immediate problem. Information-searching may be motivated by other goals such as a desire to learn, which is not simply reducible to instrumental educational goals. However, what it emphasised is the fact that central to successful information-literacy programmes is the generation of critical skills which allow the individual to critically reflect on the information obtained, and to consequently effectively deploy the information to generate new ideas or knowledge. Lennox and Walker (1993: 315) sum this up as follows.

> ... inherent in the definition of information literacy is the ability to dissect and understand what is seen and heard [and read – *not in original*]. If we are to teach information literacy, we must teach students to question, sort, discriminate, select and analyse the array of messages that are presented in traditional or electronic formats, and then to reassemble the parts into new and meaningful wholes.

This call is emphasised in the paper by Makhubela and Koen (1995), where they reiterate the need in historically disadvantaged institutions in South Africa to teach students not just how to use the library but also how to analyse critically and to evaluate the information they obtain.

Information literacy and changing perspectives on teaching and learning: A new learner-centered, lifelong learning paradigm?

The generation of critical cognitive skills, which is central to definitions of literacy, implies for many writers a change in the way the teaching-learning dynamic is conceived. Whereas traditional notions of teaching and learning have been lecturer-led and text-book-centered, the impact of new information technologies requires that learning is conceived not as transmission of information but rather as the generation of critical skills in learners to search for, evaluate and use information. This implies that learning should be learner-centered with the focus on guiding and directing learners to ways of solving problems or acquiring understanding rather than prescribing or limiting students to single sources of information.

Teaching and learning thus cannot be left to transmitting information since this is virtually unlimited, nor can it be solely dependent upon the instructor, since there are multiple sources of information. If this is true, then information literacy, according to various writers, should be directed towards showing people "how" and "why" rather than "what". By empowering learners to be self-directed and independent, it is argued that this allows them to engage in learning beyond the confines of the formal instructional setting. Providing learners with the skills to engage in lifelong learning allows them to respond to information throughout their lives and enable them to be active citizens.

"... learning should ... focus on guiding and directing learners to ways of solving problems ..."

Bruce (1995: 165) captures this shift in the following way:

> ... strategies such as contract, resource-based, and problem-based learning are more suitable than traditional lecture and tutorial based courses. Courses falling into the latter category need to focus on using assignments, or other elements that encourage independent learning, to foster information literacy.

The above definition aptly synthesises what many (for example, Ford 1994; Rader 1995) argue to be the key educational challenge of the 21st century, namely the need to move from content to process and the need to equip students with skills to use information independently, rather than to rely on the teacher/lecturer. Information literacy is thus central to the restructuring of educational thought and policies (Adams and Bailey 1993) and an important factor in enhancing the quality of life of the learner (Marais 1994: 14).

Enabling students to become independent learners implies that they are prepared and equipped to learn throughout their lives. This notion of lifelong learning is slightly distinct from that articulated in the South African context, which includes the notion of permanent learning but which particularly emphasises access to learning for those who have, due to the apartheid system of education, been denied educational opportunities. However, it shares with the South African definition the need for "a more comprehensive and visionary concept which includes formal, non-formal and informal learning extended throughout the life-span of an individual to attain the fullest possible development in personal, social and professional life" (National Education Policy Investigation 1993: 8).

Information literacy and knowledge

Many of the definitions of information literacy do not make a distinction between the concepts of information and knowledge. Often these two concepts are either used interchangeably or the notion of information subsumes that of knowledge. Many definitions assume that learners who are able to critically evaluate and use information are able to generate knowledge. While this is true, it is analytically useful to make the distinction between information and knowledge. Information is inert and passive, whereas knowledge generation is a creative process requiring active engagement and critical thinking skills.

This distinction between information and knowledge resonates with the expansive notion of information literacy articulated by Karelse and Underwood (1996). They argue that information is not neutral and that information-literacy work should alert learners to the politics of information generation. Thus, their argument implies that information literacy is about the ability to be critical and reflexive, a key condition for knowledge production. The distinction between information and knowledge and the argument concerning the politically-imbued nature of information underscores the point that mastery of information-literacy skills is an integrated part of an active, learner-engaged process of generating knowledge in the context of higher education.

"Information is inert and passive, whereas knowledge generation is a creative process ..."

Normative orientations in the definitions

A key characteristic of most, if not all, definitions of information literacy is that they are normatively orientated (this begs the obvious question of whether any definition can be "absent" from a normative orientation). Information literacy is presumed to be directed towards, for example, the creation of independent learners or non-transmission modes of teaching. Two key normative orientations are prominent. Firstly, information literacy should generate civic-minded and knowledgeable citizens who are able to access and utilise information in order to enhance their civil participation. This idea is captured in the following quotation: "... information literacy is and will be essential to a citizenry to prepare to participate in the political decision making that affects their lives ..." (Lennox and Walker 1993: 316).

Secondly, information literacy is central to economic development and growth both of the individual and the company (or country). Thus, the acquisition of information literacy is particularly vital in ensuring economic empowerment for the individual and economic prosperity for a nation. This is best expressed by the following quotation:

"... the acquisition of information literacy is particularly vital in ensuring economic empowerment for the individual and economic prosperity for a nation."

> Information literacy ... is an awareness of the growing role of the technological enablers that allow a company to re-engineer the entire business process ... information literacy involves an understanding that competitive business performance is based on an appreciation of the

critical nature of information whether it be computer based or not. (Kanter 1995: 7)

Normative orientations in definitions of information literacy resonate with the claims advanced by Karelse and Underwood (1996) that information is not value-free. Thus, information-literacy work presupposes notions of what is desirable and is therefore not reducible to basic skills acquisition, a prevailing tendency in much of the current literature.

Characteristics of an information-literate person

The definitions of information literacy reviewed above implicitly presume certain characteristics and qualities which an information-literate person should possess. This set of skills is best expressed by Breivik as follows:

- Understand processes for acquiring information, including systems for information identification and delivery;
- Can evaluate the effectiveness of various information channels;
- Master basic skills in acquiring and storing their own information;
- Are articulate, responsible citizens in considering public policy issues relating to information (1987: 46/7).

The key characteristics are the ability of learners to access, evaluate and use information. However, as is pointed out in the following section, these definitions omit consideration of factors such as contextually located learning (or "situated cognition") and the student's prior learning experiences.

Factors absent in the definitions

The definitions of information literacy reviewed above highlight the key concerns of the information-literacy movement. In particular, they emphasise the need to move away from narrow bibliographic instruction programmes and from a perception that information-skills training is in the domain of librarians. Instead, they signal that a more holistic approach to education in which librarians, academics and others collaborate in generating cross-curricular programmes.

However, the definitions of information literacy reviewed above do not always pay sufficient attention to certain issues which are crucial in developing a fuller understanding of the concept in the South African context. These are:

Attention to context

Most definitions of information literacy ignore the context in which learning and teaching takes place and assume an "equity" among students in terms of access to (educational) resources. These factors also include the history and tradition of institutions, departments and faculties, infrastructure and resource issues, and the disciplinary orientations and frameworks within which teaching and learning takes place. Information literacy is therefore as much about the resources and materials that frame the nature and form of information as it is about higher-order cognitive skills.

Information literacy and access

Many definitions of information literacy underplay the fact that central to the successful implementation of information-literacy programmes and to the acquisition of such skills is access to the relevant information technologies and materials. This is not always the case for all learners, particularly in the South African higher-education sector where historically disadvantaged institutions have been denied and deprived of the necessary resources which facilitate connection and supply access to various information technologies. For example, most historically disadvantaged institutions have poor library holdings and computer facilities, making information access difficult. Notions of information literacy from the developed world often take for granted basic facilities and resources which simply do not exist in South Africa. Successful information literacy tuition, as Makhubela and Koen (1995: 18) note in their conclusion, is as much about the library resources and facilities at UWC, as it is about changing approaches to learning.

"... most historically disadvantaged institutions have poor library holdings and computer facilities, making information access difficult."

Information literacy and prior learning

Many definitions of information literacy do not take into account the learner's prior learning experiences. The definitions assume that all learners are homogeneous and that they are all equal when they enter higher-education institutions. Thus, not many of the definitions refer to the experiences of learning that learners bring to bear as they access, evaluate and use information in the higher-education context. In South Africa it is important to take cognisance of the effect of apartheid education on learners, particularly in designing programmes geared towards enhancing information literacy.

South African voices on information literacy

As part of the process of arriving at an operational definition that would be recognised and "owned" by service providers and other role players on all the Calico campuses, it was decided to consult with key informants from all five institutions, to arrive at a common understanding and definition of information literacy (see Chapter 3). The perceived advantage of these discussions was that they would provide a forum for people to develop a collective view of the subject and to obtain an operational definition of information literacy. This definition was then used to guide and inform the design of questionnaires and interviews for the research team's investigation into information literacy at the five institutions.

Describing information literacy

The first question, which asked for expressions of how information literacy is understood, generally produced responses that were highly consistent with the literature in the field. This illustrated the extent to which the participants were involved and grappling with issues relating to information literacy and indicated that they had been correctly identified as key informants.

Respondents readily agreed that information-literacy skills were not to be narrowly defined, but that they consisted of a combination of library skills, computer skills, media skills and traditional literacy skills, functioning within a context of being able to make productive and competent use of retrieved information. One group succinctly expressed that an information-literate person was one who could recognise an information need, knew where to look for information, had the necessary skills to access that information from a selection of sources, was able to evaluate the information obtained and then could use and communicate the obtained information to others: a definition highly consistent with that found in the Information Literacy Blueprint from Australia (Bruce 1994). Another group contributed the useful insight that it could be problematic to settle for too rigid a definition, as information literacy is not only highly dependent on context, but that the access tools and approaches to information are in a constant state of flux and development and should not be pegged down by fixed definitions. A need was expressed for a "durable" and flexible definition that would remain relevant in spite of rapidly shifting contexts and technologies.

This group was particularly concerned with the information-technology component of information literacy and the importance of the computer as the tool for managing information. While some members of the group seemed to imply that mastering information technology was the most significant aspect of becoming information literate, one member of the group expressed the conviction that printed tools and sources may be more appropriate in satisfying certain information needs. While this was accepted, there was support for the speaker who declared that printed books would ultimately become too expensive to be sustained and that computers will be the information tools of the future.

The groups agreed that information literacy was a lifelong process that developed throughout a student's career. It is not an attribute that only pertains to an academic elite, but life-enhancing skills that all students should be empowered to obtain.

Information-handling skills

A question about the actual skills required to be an information-literate person produced a lengthy discussion in the first group, which served to enrich the research team's understanding of information literacy in the specific context of South African academic disadvantage. It was emphasised that information literacy consisted of an "infusion" of various different skills, many of which may be taken for granted by teachers and lecturers, but which students simply do not possess. "Recognising an information need", for example, includes having to know what the use or purpose of information could be. Not only are students unfamiliar with libraries and computers, they are often unaware that a whole range of other information sources also "count", such as newspapers, films, videos, the telephone, the Yellow Pages, their experiences and other people.

Students have difficulty in knowing how and where to start a search for information and do not realise that it is unlikely that there would be a single source containing all the answers. Simply repackaging information to make finding it easier, was regarded with suspicion by the interviewees, as students may then rely too much on the repackaged material and never become information literate.

Reading skills were regarded as an essential component of information literacy; students should be able to decode a text meaningfully. Some find it difficult, for example, to recognise "voices", to know when an author is expressing an opinion, or whether someone else is being quoted. "Reading between the lines", or understanding what is suggested rather than overtly stated, is problematic, as are the numeracy skills required, for example, in obtaining useful information from a graph or chart. It was emphasised that information literacy was not a skill that could simply be taught; it was an experiential process, which could only be acquired by much practising.

"Reading skills were regarded as an essential component of information literacy; students should be able to decode a text meaningfully."

One group suggested that the acquisition of information literacy was not a natural process, but that it was built upon in the first place through learning the specific language and terminology of a subject field. Such subject skills, however, had to be coupled with data processing and technological skills, as the ability to access information through a variety of technological tools also formed an essential aspect of information literacy. In addition, remaining information literate after higher education might require new learning, the acquisition of different skills in the use of the latest electronic tools and much more effort to stay abreast of information in a specific field.

The importance of higher-order cognitive skills was emphasised by two of the groups. The skill of distilling relevance, for example, is critical in view of the rapidly shifting contexts and vast amounts of information "out there" which students have to navigate. "Thinking skills" such as being able to evaluate critically, to sift, assess and source information, have to be gained by experiential learning and practice and cannot be trivialised by attempts to pin them down as single, teachable skills.

It was also noted that affective factors play a significant role in the acquisition of information literacy. Without confidence or motivation, or even "natural curiosity", students would not be able to deal effectively with a recognised information need.

Relationship between information literacy and knowledge production

One group spent some time exploring the relationship between information literacy and knowledge production. It was suggested that information literacy was the ultimate aim of all higher education – to produce people immersed in the conceptual framework, the terminology, philosophy and methodology of a subject, and who were equipped with the tools allowing them to maintain currency and to continue educating themselves in that field after leaving the educational institution. The group therefore spent some time discussing the use of the word "literacy" and whether the discussion was suggesting that the concept "information literacy" was so broad and all-inclusive as to be of little value in definition.

In defending the use of the term in this context, it was argued that traditional literacy did not simply concern the ability to read and write, but was crucially associated with the social practices surrounding language. Information literacy therefore included knowing how knowledge was organised and how to reproduce or generate new knowledge. Information-literate people are able to write or to share; to produce new knowledge and to communicate to others the products of their active learning.

This communication or reproduction of knowledge might take place in a variety of ways. One of the groups especially emphasised that oral cultures and traditions should be recognised alongside that of the printed, written word which was in any case now being challenged by the much more ephemeral nature of the electronic text. Information-literate people are able to move easily and confidently between information sources and know what to do with information once it has been found.

The contextualisation of information literacy

All the groups considered the question of the contextualisation of information-literacy skills: whether information literacy is a generic attribute which may be regarded as the goal of all higher education or whether it is context- or discipline-specific. Were information-literacy skills best taught as a separate course on the understanding that they were transferable skills which, once learnt, could be applied in any situation, or was it best to teach them in some course-specific context?

Two groups noted that aspects of information literacy were not context-sensitive, that the world no longer was as discipline-driven as in the past and that there might well be a "general communicative competence" that could be taught in an interdisciplinary approach. Several interviewees, however, expressed the conviction that these skills where not necessarily transferable; that the information skills required by a student in the fine arts, for example, were vastly different from those required by a student in physics or chemistry. It was recognised that all teaching of information literacy needs to address common issues such as coverage, currency and validity in order to impart certain generic, transferable skills, but it was also accepted that this teaching cannot successfully take place outside a specific subject area and without using the language or terminology of that subject.

After considerable discussion, both groups tended to agree that information-literacy skills were best acquired within the context of a specific subject. It was felt that information literacy cannot be divorced from the discourse of a subject field, as one required an understanding of the specific language and terminology associated with a subject in order to comprehend an information need and recognise relevant information. This conforms to the argument of Karelse and Underwood (1996) who argue that the acquisition of information literacy is context- or domain-specific.

The first group confirmed that, while information literacy skills were best learnt and practised within a specific subject, they would be learnt even better if they were taught within a number of different subjects. It was also noted that information-literacy skills might be taught more effectively when they are "silently infused" and not openly present in the curriculum. Another group seemed to suggest that the facilitator should be conscious of nurturing information literacy in learners, without necessarily making it overt.

An important aspect of the contextualisation of the concept of information literacy that emerged, was the recognition of the importance of the particularly South African context. The pilot interview had provided the research team with the insight that students currently in the five institutions exhibit a wide diversity of backgrounds and that an effective, student-centred approach to learning would have to take into consideration the prior learning experiences that the students brought with them. Such more flexible approach to learning will also take into consideration that a student's own experience could be a legitimate information resource.

> "It was felt that information literacy cannot be divorced from the discourse of a subject field ..."

Factors that enhance information literacy

It was recognised that a number of existing courses at the three universities and two technikons teach aspects of what may be called information literacy, even though the courses themselves might bear no evidence of that terminology. The extent to which this is done, is frequently related to the resources that are available. It was, however, felt that not a great deal of explicit information literacy-skills teaching was going on outside the libraries, where much of it still took place in the guise of bibliographic instruction, and in the departments of academic development, where these issues were of major concern.

Two of the groups were convinced that a paradigm shift was required before the institutions could be able to claim that they aimed to produce students who were truly information-literate. Most courses at present were lecturer-centered and lecturer-dependent, in the traditional mould where the lecturer is regarded as the source of all the knowledge needed by the student in order to qualify.

"... students currently in the five institutions exhibit a wide diversity of backgrounds and ... an effective, student-centred approach to learning would have to take into consideration the prior learning experiences ..."

Students therefore have to become more dynamically engaged in their own learning and have to be actively exposed to a range of information sources appropriate for their specific disciplines. The critical, defining feature of an information-literacy focus to teaching and learning, the groups thought, was a shift to a mode that was more student-centered, with the aim of producing students that were not only immersed in their subjects, but confident about productively using a variety of information tools and sources specific to those subjects. Partnerships between librarians and teachers were seen to be crucial in this regard.

Many obstacles to a paradigm shift of this nature were noted. It was emphasised that such a shift had significant budgetary implications and that a commitment to redefine an institution as a learning organisation had to be championed by the top management structure in the first place. Only involvement at this level would ensure that the resources required for the implementation of change (such as the provision of infrastructure providing all learners with access to electronic information resources) would be available. Anxiety was expressed at the rapidity with which tools and technologies were changing, while institutions were faced with increasing resource constraints and the inability to provide general access to the latest tools and technologies for both undergraduate and post-graduate students at an institution.

One of the groups was particularly concerned with obstacles from the learners themselves. Often students, especially from disadvantaged backgrounds, come to higher education with a dualistic world view and expect to be provided with the "correct" answers or with specific texts. They find it very threatening to be presented with different points of view and a lecturer's expectation that they should be able to distil and defend an individual position. Such students were satisfied with and indeed demanded reading lists and course readers. They do not wish to explore the world of information by themselves, while lecturers generally provide very little assistance in an activity which they regard as the student's own responsibility.

It was agreed that successful information-literacy courses at present were those with limited but achievable objectives, which were learning-centered, integrated into specific subject courses, activity-focused and which essentially attempted to effect a transformation by empowering students to take charge of their own learning. In addition, all the groups emphasised that the acquisition of information literacy was a developmental and indeed a lifelong process that cannot be taught once and for all or in a fairly brief period.

Approaches to a definition

Both the literature review and the interviews strongly suggest that it is problematic to achieve a definition of the notion of information literacy that readily lends itself to practical application. It was however possible to identify various sub-concepts and factors relating to the definition of information literacy in general and with specific reference to South Africa. These are:

- *Prior learning experiences:* In defining information literacy, attention needs to be paid to the fact that students from vastly under-resourced educational systems have not been exposed to information sources and technologies that require or foster the development of information literacy. Thus learners bring differing educational experiences to teaching and learning environments at the higher-education level. This also implies that attention should be focused on the linguistic competence of learners which have a bearing on their ability to access and utilise information resources.

- *Contextually-specific teaching and learning:* Any definition of information literacy in South Africa should take into account various contextual features of the South African higher-education system that impinge on teaching and learning. These include, inter alia, the fact that educational technology resources are unevenly distributed across the five institutions in the Western Cape province.

- *Affective issues:* Any definition of information literacy must incorporate the understanding that learners are able to recognise when they have an information need, and are confident and motivated to explore the world of information to fulfil such needs.

- *Access skills:* Allied to motivation, information literacy presumes that learners possess the necessary skills and abilities to access information from various sources. This includes the library, electronic databases and computer networks. For this to be possible, learners should possess various literacies such as computer literacy and library literacy.

- *Use and evaluation:* Having identified and accessed appropriate and relevant sources of information, information literacy denotes a learner's ability to critically evaluate and use the information to solve problems, accomplish tasks and generate new ideas.

- *Higher-order cognitive skills:* Critical evaluation and manipulation of information implies that learners possess higher-order

"... successful information-literacy courses at present were those with limited but achievable objectives ..."

cognitive skills which enable them to generate new ideas and contribute to knowledge production.

■ *Student-centered learning:* Central to the definition of information literacy is the assumption that with the advent of new information technologies and the vast amounts of information that are available, teaching and learning should be directed towards making learners independent and teaching them how rather than what to learn. This implies that educators should see themselves as facilitators and guides through a process instead of sages possessing all information and knowledge.

The above summarises the salient points relating to the notion of information literacy that has emerged from the basic research. From this an possible operational definition of the concept emerged which was used as the baseline from which to develop the research instruments:

> Information literacy refers to the ability of learners to access, use and evaluate information from different sources, in order to enhance learning, solve problems and generate new knowledge.

This definition must be understood in the context of the following, namely that in South African higher education, information literacy develops when situational and affective factors that impinge upon the teaching and learning process are recognised by learners and teachers alike. Information literacy is most effectively imparted in an environment which is centered around the learner rather than the teacher in a collaborative relationship which also includes other facilitators such as librarians, and specialists in computer applications and academic development. The development of information literacy is directed towards producing independent and self-directed learners who are able to become active and responsible citizens, make informed decisions in their private and public lives and contribute to both individual and national empowerment and growth.

"... educators should see themselves as facilitators and guides through a process, instead of sages possessing all information and knowledge."

This definition, in conjunction with the contextual issues as outlined above, captures the major insights that have emerged from the investigation. The above working definition was used as the basis upon which to develop the questionnaires and the interview schedule for the research.

The following chapter discusses the concept of information literacy in relation to both the South African context and two comparative examples, namely those of Australia and Malaysia.

2

Information Literacy in a Comparative Context

This chapter contextualises the debate on information literacy by reviewing local and global trends in the debate. It also summarises key insights gleaned from a study visit to Malaysia and Australia.

The South African context

The impact of new information technologies on society in general and education in particular has been recognised in South Africa in, for example, the report of the Working Group on Libraries and Information Technologies (WGLIT) to the National Commission on Higher Education and the Technology-Enhanced Learning Investigation commissioned by the Department of Education. The WGLIT report focuses on the impact of information technologies on learning in higher education and consequently the changing role of libraries. The latter report focuses on the impact of information technologies on the school system.

In general, both reports argue that global information changes necessitate a rethink and reorientation of the South African education system in order to ensure economic and human-resource development. They both contend that new information technologies make possible new and innovative approaches to teaching and learning. However, both reports caution against an uncritical belief and utilisation of information technology in the learning context. The key findings of the two reports can be summarised as follows:

- The application and utilisation of information technologies (ITs) in the education system must be part of an overall co-ordinated IT strategy that is rooted in the specificity of the South African situation.
- The changes in information technologies necessitate information-literacy programmes that contribute directly to the promotion of a learning society and an information community.
- Infrastructural support is vital in maximising the potential of the new information technologies. However, this is a necessary but not sufficient condition for information literacy. Infrastructural support and investment must be accompanied by changes in the teaching and learning approaches. These changes include collapsing of boundaries between libraries and

"The promotion of information-literacy skills and abilities ... requires co-operative ventures and partnerships between education institutions and the Department of Education ... (as well as) other actors such as the private sector."

IT departments; the integration of libraries and academic programmes; the move towards multi- and intra-disciplinary programmes; the recognition that the products of education, specifically higher education, should not only acquire content and disciplinary knowledge. They should also have the necessary attributes of an information-literate person, namely the ability to access and critically use and evaluate information, life-long learning skills, social skills which promote co-operative work and the flexibility to adapt to new environments.

■ The promotion of information-literacy skills and abilities and the utilisation of new technologies requires co-operative ventures and partnerships between education institutions and the Department of Education, between education institutions/ departments and other actors such as the private sector.

■ The commitment to redress and human-resource development should accompany any moves towards investment in and the development of appropriate new information technologies.

A key recommendation of the report by the National Commission on Higher Education was the need for a thorough investigation of IT facilities at the higher-education level. The study undertaken by the Infolit project dovetails with this recommendation by focusing on the state of information literacy at the five higher-education institutions in the Western Cape region.

Two specific examples – Malaysia and Australia

During the course of the investigation into information literacy in the region, a study visit of Malaysia and Australia was undertaken. The purpose of this visit was to view how the two countries responded to changing and new forms of information technologies. Some of the key issues that emerged from the visit are highlighted here.

Context of information literacy in the two countries

Malaysia, as a fast growing economy in the East, and Australia, positioning itself as a regional power in the Pacific, both strongly emphasise and respond to the advent of emerging forms of information technology.

The visit to Malaysia revealed two significant trends. Firstly, discussion regarding information technology and literacy is inextricably linked to issues of economic development and the stated strategy for growth and progress as identified in the Seventh Malaysia Plan (1996–2001). Information literacy is thus part of a process of ensuring that the Malaysian economy continues to grow and that it remains internationally highly competitive. In addition, information literacy is a strategy to modernise society and in particular departments and agencies of the government. In this respect, the Malaysian Administrative Modernisation and

Management Planning Unit argued that a key influence of information technology in the country was the move towards a paperless bureaucracy where much of the information will be captured electronically, thus eliminating paperwork. In fact, projects which reduce bureaucratic and administrative paper overload are awarded grants by government.

In Malaysia, the promotion and advocacy for information technology and literacy was not only part of a centrally initiated and co-ordinated strategy; it was also spearheaded by the president. The influence and moves towards greater information sensitivity is thus a result of the efforts of the president and his advisors. For example, the new information highway – the Multi-Media Super-Corridor – to be established in Kuala Lumpur is a direct result of the president's championing of the cause in which he drew in Bill Gates from Microsoft as a consultant.

It is evident in Malaysia that higher-education institutions are beginning to respond to the new information technologies. This includes new programmes with an explicit information-technology bias and short in-service programmes/courses that develop information-literacy skills. An example of this is the M.Ed. in information technology offered by the Faculty of Education of the University of Malaysia. This phenomenon is also beginning to surface in schools with the ministry claiming that they will soon be offering a compulsory course in information technology at Form Six level, and that an outcome of primary schooling in Malaysia, is pupils who are aware and responsive to information-technology. It is also envisaged in the near future, that all university students will take an information-technology foundation course related to their field of study.

The Australian picture suggests a strong commitment to information literacy, in part a consequence of the realisation of the growth of new information technologies. This was evident in the growing commitment of most higher-education institutions in Brisbane in promoting programmes that enhance information-literacy skills and use. For example, the Queensland University Library Office of Co-operation, an informal consortium of mainly librarians but also academics, meets regularly to exchange ideas and information regarding information literacy.

At the higher-education level universities in the Brisbane region have begun the process of institutionalising the moves towards the acquisition of information-literacy skills. This occurs at two levels. Firstly, most higher-education institutions regard the ability to access, use and evaluate information to be a critical outcome and competency to be acquired by learners graduating from higher-education institutions. This seems to be the case in most Australian higher-education institutions. Secondly, some institutions have made information literacy a central component of institutional life. Griffiths University has developed an Information-Literacy Blueprint which can be perceived to represent an

"The spread and increased use of appropriate information technologies is ... central to the projects of catapulting Malaysian society into the 21st century."

information-technology mission statement. In addition, there is a growing number of programmes which are consciously designed to promote information-literacy skills. These are, however, still optional or are additional courses to the traditional university offerings.

Discourses of information literacy

The interviews revealed that information literacy and information technology are buzz-words that are often invoked on the grounds that it is good to mention them. However, it is evident that there are differing and possibly competing discourses regarding information literacy.

At the semantic level, it is evident that whereas persons in Australia continuously invoked the notion of information literacy, this was not the case in Malaysia. Here the word "information technology" were principally used and the word "information literacy" were rarely cited in discussions. Why this is the case is difficult to understand. The reason seems to be Malaysia's emphasis on development of the information infrastructure (hence the "information-technology" focus), but even more importantly the apparent belief that through making the technology transparent, people will become information-literate and able to function fluently in the information society. It seems that there is almost a conflation of information literacy and information-technology literacy.

In Malaysia the notion of information literacy is constituted in the domain of modernisation and economic development. The spread and increased use of appropriate information technologies is perceived to be central to the projects of catapulting Malaysian society into the 21st century. Information technologies are perceived to have wide-ranging applications in how the business of government is conducted. As mentioned earlier, the work of the Malaysian Administrative Modernisation and Management Planning Unit is illustrative of this trend. Allied to the modernisation project is the growing assumption that technological familiarity and competence among all Malaysians is central to the continued economic development of the country and vital in ensuring that Malaysia develops as the economic power-house in the East.

In the discourses of information literacy the notion of appropriate and relevant information technology continually surfaces. Emphasis is placed on the fact that for society and citizens to develop, it is necessary to pay due attention to seeking information technologies that are appropriate to the needs and problems identified. This was contrasted with information-technology fetishism where the latest technologies are imported and purchased which are often not necessary and extravagant.

At the educational level, information literacy (despite the different semantic constructions between the two countries) was identified with the moves to refocus teaching and learning away from teacher-dominated instructional setting towards more learner-centered and resource-based education. The discourse of learner-centered education is premised on the grounds that new information technologies generate multiple sources of informational resources which cannot be "taught" in the conventional lecture-student relationship. Instead, it is argued that learning, particularly at the higher-education level, should provide students with generic competencies and skills which enable them to become effective information-seekers and critical users. Such an approach to learning, it is believed, necessitates greater collaboration between academics, librarians and other persons involved in education. As such, the move towards a learner-centered environment requires a redefinition and reorientation of all those involved in the education sector.

Models and initiatives for developing an information-literacy culture

Most of the models evidenced in Australia were library-initiated and library-driven. These were mimicked to a greater or lesser extent in Malaysia. This library-orientation is most likely a result of the fact that hosts were in the main librarians and seldom people involved in programmes like the Academic Staff Development Unit at the Queensland University of Technology or its equivalents, the Centre for Teaching and Learning at the University of Technology Sydney or the Griffiths Institute of Higher Education at Griffiths University. The models found in Malaysia were government-wide initiatives which, as explained earlier, are primed at generating both an information and a learning culture through the infusion of information technology in all aspects of the society.

"Such an approach to learning, it is believed, necessitates greater collaboration between academics, librarians and other persons involved in education."

The approach to information literacy in Malaysia, as was noted, is seen as an automatic part of information-society development. For this reason the models found, apart from the information-skills courses similar to those found in Australia, were largely infused into broader initiatives to bring the country onto the information highway. The strong assumption made in all the models is that as people become familiar and comfortable with information technology, so they will develop an information culture which will generate critical thinking and a consciousness about knowledge production. For example, the National Librarian spoke about efforts to involve citizens in documenting the cultural heritage of the country through Adult Literacy and Children's Educational Programmes facilitated by her institution.

The models which were distinct from those found in Australia operate mainly at school level, but this includes polytechnics and teacher's training colleges. The primary focus in Malaysia is to facilitate a culture of development. Five key aspects central to this culture are identified, namely people, training, rules/policy, technology and finance.

The country is alert to the problem of information-society development reinforcing historical divides and are reluctant to reproduce an elite minority. For this reason, the state subsidises technological infrastructural development in rural areas and in poorer communities, while parent-teacher associations and institutions are expected to sponsor such development in more affluent schools.

The education ministry in collaboration with the government and within the framework of Vision 2020, Malaysia's plan for growth and development for the 21st century, has embarked on a programme to integrate information technology into education at a primary and secondary level. Throughout the programmes, rural schools have been prioritised to ensure their inclusion in the development process.

Factors facilitating information-literacy development

The case-studies of Australia and Malaysia suggest that the success of information literacy in schools and at the higher-education levels is dependent on a number of enabling policy conditions. Four critical factors are identified:

Central/high-level endorsement

In Malaysia it was clear that the extent to which information literacy became entrenched and institutionalised was dependent upon high-level endorsement and advocacy. Presidential support for the promotion of the use of information technology made possible a number of initiatives in the field.

By contrast, in Australia there were continual complaints that the spread of information literacy was not as wide as desired and expected, partly because there was not a strong push from, for example, those occupying senior positions in higher-education institutions. The Brisbane approach tended to focus on small initiatives and work by like-minded people with the hope that as such initiatives grew and gained recognition, so would the promotion of information literacy.

Collaborative and co-operative relationships/networks

In both Malaysia and Australia collaboration was perceived to be vital to the successful institutionalisation of information-literacy projects and programmes. Persons spoken to continually emphasised that good information literacy required sustainable co-operative relationships in which traditional boundaries and divisions were broken down. Forms of collaboration in the two countries vary and include partnerships between, inter alia, academics and information specialists; academics, information specialists and government departments such as the ministry of education; government departments, business and interested groups/persons who formed either strongly co-ordinated or loosely associated networks and structures.

"Throughout the programmes, rural schools have been prioritised to ensure their inclusion in the development process."

Cultural and political symbols

In order to effect a change in educational emphasis towards greater information-literacy awareness and sensitivity it was important to have symbols in place which signalled the change. For example, the Griffiths University Blueprint was considered to be a suitable information-literacy mission statement which could rally and mobilise institutions to pursue activities in the field. Symbolic imaging is an effective strategy for the purpose of institutionalising change to enhance information-literacy projects and programmes.

Creating appropriate institutional structures and frameworks

Perhaps the strongest impression conveyed from the visits was the need to create institutional structures and frameworks which work towards successful information-literacy implementations. Again, the creation of a Division of Information Literacy at Griffiths University provides a structural focal point for the dissemination and propagation of information-literacy work. In Malaysia the creation of a Division of Information Technology in the ministry of education enabled educators to begin implementing awareness and competency information-technology programmes and projects in schools. Without the necessary institutional structures and frameworks, it was not always possible to provide a unit which strategises, initiates, implements and monitors information-literacy work. In addition, the absence of such structures did not advance co-operation and partnership between interested persons/groups nor did it make lobbying possible and easy.

Human resource capacity to deliver information-literacy programmes

A key issue identified from the visit was that the successful institutionalisation of information literacy requires persons who are skilled to effect this. Both countries expressed concern over the limited availability of human capacity to deliver and sustain information-literacy programmes. In particular, it was argued that there is a paucity of individuals who are

- sensitive to and aware of the new information technologies,
- technically competent to master these technologies, and, more importantly,
- in possession of the necessary educational training to integrate the new information technologies in ways which make student-centered learning possible.

Thus, in both countries human-resource development was identified to be a key priority. Furthermore, it was affirmed that education and training of persons as independent and able to use new information technologies effectively is central to developing the country's person-power potential. Thus the new information

"... there is a paucity of individuals who are ... 'sensitive to and aware of the new information technologies' ..."

"... information-literacy skills require changing approaches to teaching and learning, and active commitment by governments and departments to information-literacy practice."

technologies are perceived as underscoring the need for a human-resource-development strategy which trains people to cope with working in the information age and also trains the trainers to effect this.

Conclusion

This chapter has provided a national and international contextualisation of the information-literacy debate. Key issues which have been highlighted include the fact that mastering of technology is a necessary but not sufficient condition for the acquisition of information literacy. Furthermore, information-literacy skills require changing approaches to teaching and learning and active commitment by governments and departments to information-literacy practice.

The following chapter outlines the research process undertaken in the investigation into mapping levels of information literacy in the higher-education sector in the region.

3

Research Design and Methodology[*]

The chapter highlights the various stages of the research process from review of the definition(s) of the concept of information literacy to the analysis of the data.

Research design

The study utilised a combination of quantitative and qualitative research methods. A questionnaire survey was conducted of a representative sample of students at the five higher-education institutions. The questionnaire survey assessed student's information-literacy abilities and needs.

Focus-group interviews provided an opportunity to discuss with key informants at the five institutions aspects regarding information literacy. Two sets of focus-group interviews were held. The first was about the understandings of the notion of information literacy. The second discussed the preliminary findings obtained from the questionnaires regarding students' information-literacy abilities and needs.[1]

Process towards an understanding of information literacy

As has been outlined in the previous chapter, an important first step in the study was to generate a definition of information literacy which could be used to guide the project. This definition was also critical in the design of the questionnaires which assessed information literacy at the five institutions in the province.

The development of the definition of information literacy involved two related processes. Firstly, a review of literature published from 1992 to 1995 was conducted. The literature review provided an understanding of the many definitions of the concept of information literacy (see Chapter 2). Secondly, focus-group interviews were conducted with key informants at the five institutions. Strategic informants were selected from the libraries, from academic-development programmes, from information-technology services

---

[*] Where total percentages in tables, graphs and charts have been rounded off, totals deviate slightly.

and also academics who had in the past expressed an interest in aspects of information literacy and/or who were considered to be knowledgeable in the field. Some thirty key informants were identified and twenty-seven eventually attended one of the three focus-group interviews.

Before the start of the focus-group sessions, one pilot interview was held, consisting of a discussion of the draft-interview schedule with an expert in the field of academic development. The discussion lasted for three quarters of an hour and provided a useful framework for the interviews that were to follow.

Three focus-group interviews were held, each attended by between eight and ten interviewees. The interviews were held on three different campuses and representatives from at least two different institutions were present at each. No attempt was made to group the interviewees according to discipline or interest, as it was considered important to gain the opinions from as broad a cross chapter of informants as possible. The interviews were tape-recorded and the same interview schedule was used in each case. The schedule consisted of, *inter alia*, the following questions:

■ What do you understand by the term "information literacy"?
■ What do you therefore regard as the distinguishing features of an information-literate person?
■ Which programmes/projects at your institution or in your experience may qualify as projects or programmes that will enhance information literacy in students?
■ Please list what you would regard as the key characteristics of information-literacy programmes.

Designing the research instruments

Drawing upon the work concerning the generation of an operational definition of the concept of information literacy, the research team designed an approximate questionnaire. The first entitled "Questionnaire to Students on Information Literacy" consisted of five sections with 70 items (see Appendix). This questionnaire consisted of mainly closed questions. The five sections dealt with different aspects of the concept of information literacy identified in the initial phase of the study, *inter alia,* learning background and prior learning experiences (sections 1 and 2), students' orientation and predisposition to information literacy (section 3), students' competence and needs in respect of different sources of information (section 4) and students' perception and rating of lecturing/teaching approaches (section 5). The students' questionnaire employed different response formats. These included a three-point scale (often, sometimes, never), a categorical response scale (yes/no) and a semantic differential scale where students were asked to rate their responses to a series of statements on a scale of 1 to 5.

The questionnaire specifically obtained information considered to have an important bearing on information-literacy competencies in the South African context. Thus, students were asked to provide information concerning their home language, race, age and gender. The analysis of the data (see chapters 5, 6 and 7) specifically reports on the relationship between these factors and information-literacy abilities and needs.

The questionnaire included open-ended questions which were attached at the end. The open-ended questions asked students and lecturers for their views on information literacy.

The questionnaire was piloted prior to its actual administration. It was given to selected students. The feedback from students was incorporated into the final draft. In addition, the questionnaire was given to the research-resource group for the study. They made useful and relevant suggestions. The research advisory board was involved throughout the course of the study from the point of formal conceptualisation of the study to the final writing of the book.

Sampling[2]

The sampling strategy was based upon selecting a proportional sample of students from each of the main faculties and schools at the five institutions. The procedure that was employed is as follows:

- The total student population of each institution was ascertained with respect to the number of undergraduate and postgraduate students. From this a sample size of approximately 10 per cent of the student population respectively across all institutions, was chosen.
- The total number of undergraduate and postgraduate students selected were then proportionally allocated to the main faculties.
- In each main faculty a subject representing the field of knowledge was chosen and the students divided proportionally into undergraduates and postgraduates.
- In each of the subjects that were chosen, the undergraduate sample was divided into the first- and third-year cohorts. The purpose of the division was to ascertain whether there was any shift in the acquisition of information-literacy skills of undergraduate students across the duration of their programmes.

"... aspects of teaching ... include ... lecturers' familiarity with and exposure to new information sources such as the Internet ..., approaches and methods of teaching ... and lecturers' perceptions of attested needs and competencies ..."

Based upon the above considerations, the following overall sample was chosen for the five institutions (the realised sample is included in the table).

TABLE 3.1: Sample of student population across the five higher-education institutions

Institutions	Student figures			Selected sample			Realised sample		
	Total	UG	PG	Total	UG	PG	Total	UG	PG
UCT	15 413	10 952	4 461	1 560	1 100	460	1 741	1 323	418
US	14 733	10 341	4 392	1 500	1 050	450	1 291	1 102	189
UWC	13 788	11 434	2 354	1 400	1 160	240	1 266	1 053	213
CT	7 752	6 565	1 187	780	660	120	570	526	44
PT	7 545	7 503	42	790	790	—	682	608	74

UG = undergraduate students   PG = postgraduate students

The table above indicates that of the 6 030 questionnaires distributed, a total of 5 629 were collected and used in the analysis. The records of total student populations are based on information supplied by the five institutions. The chosen and realised sample profiles by institution are reported in the following tables.

TABLE 3.2: Sample of student-population size for UCT

Faculty	Department	S1	S3	S4	R1	R3	R4
Sciences	Chemistry I	150			172		
	Chemistry III		60			51	
	Chemistry IV			9			—
Commerce	Economics I	220			257		
	Economics III		150			145	
	Economics IV			15			13
Arts	English I	220			249		
	English III		140			56	
	English IV			15			15
Social sciences	Psychology I	100			113		
	Psychology III		60			104	
	Psychology IV			30			22
Medicine	M.B.Ch.B. I	150			176		
	M.B.Ch.B. IV		90				117
	M.B.Ch.B. VI			153			57
Education	Education IV			80			93
Law	LL.B. IV			200			101
TOTAL		840	500	502	967	356	418

S1, 3, 4 = Selected sample size of student population for year group 1, 3, 4
R1, 3, 4 = Realised sample size of student population for year group 1, 3, 4

The sample table for UCT indicates, the sample for subjects for the year levels identified was not realised in every instance. It also shows that the postgraduate cohort mainly comprises students from the faculties of education, law and medicine.

TABLE 3.3: Sample of student-population size for US							
Faculty	**Department**	**S1**	**S3**	**S4**	**R1**	**R3**	**R4**
Sciences	Chemistry I	150			142		
	Chemistry III		30			43	
	Chemistry IV			15			—
Economics and management	Economics I	250			384		
	Economics III		130			72	
	Economics IV			70			—
Arts	English I	150			151		
	English III		75			44	
	English IV			70			6
Medicine	M.B.Ch.B. I	100			61		
	M.B.Ch.B. IV		40				81
	M.B.Ch.B. VI			60			31
Education	Education IV			60			52
Social sciences	Sociology I	120			243		
	Sociology III		50			23	
	Sociology IV			80			19
TOTAL		770	325	355	981	182	189

S1, 3, 4 = Selected sample size of student population for year group 1, 3, 4
R1, 3, 4 = Realised sample size of student population for year group 1, 3, 4

The above table indicates the low postgraduate sample realised at the US; only 189 questionnaires could be utilised out of a desired total of 450. In addition, the postgraduate sample is mainly accounted for by students in the faculty of medicine.

The sample table for UWC indicates that for most of the subjects surveyed, there was no or a very small postgraduate cohort. The postgraduate sample at UWC mainly comprises students from the faculties of education and law (147 out of 213).

The CT sample table indicates that the lowest postgraduate sample was realised there compared to the other institutions. The only postgraduate questionnaires that were obtained and used were those from the schools of engineering and management.

At PT, the postgraduate cohort comprised mainly students from the schools of education and life sciences. The gaps in the PT sample are in the disciplines of economics and management sciences and graphic design. In this respect, only first-year students were surveyed. (See tables 3.4–3.6.)

Across all five institutions, the actual realised sample was not the same as that desired for each subject. This can be attributed to the following factors.

TABLE 3.4: Sample of student-population size for UWC

Faculty	Department	S1	S3	S4	R1	R3	R4
Sciences	Chemistry I	150			53		
	Chemistry III		120			48	
	Chemistry IV			40			—
	Physics I				61		
	Physics III		120			50	
	Physics IV						—
Economics and management	Economics I	150			58		
	Economics III					73	
	Economics IV			40			3
	Financial accounting I				94		
	Financial accounting III					109	
	Financial accounting IV			40			—
Arts	English I	150			155		
	English III					103	
	English IV			40			—
Community-health sciences	Psychology I	150			161		
	Psychology III		120			88	
	Psychology IV			40			12
	Physiotherapy I	150			—		
	Physiotherapy III		120			22	
	Physiotherapy IV			40			29
Education	Theory of education IV			40			94
Law	LL.B. IV			40			53
TOTAL		750	360	320	582	493	191

S1, 3, 4 = Selected sample size of student population for year group 1, 3, 4
R1, 3, 4 = Realised sample size of student population for year group 1, 3, 4

- *A discrepancy in sample figures:* The figures provided by the various student-records departments at the institutions varied against the actual number of students enrolled in the course at the time that the questionnaires were administered. This issue was compounded by the variance in the actual numbers of students attending classes.
- *The need to avoid repetitive responses:* To avoid collating duplicated responses, students were asked not to fill in a questionnaire if they had already been approached in another class. The most significant example of this is the Physiotherapy I class at UWC, all of whom had responded in other courses such as Psychology I.
- *The cancellation of classes:* This often occurred unexpectedly, and although every attempt was made to re-schedule, limited lecture schedules and tests sometimes prevented the research team from realising figures in these cases.
- *Partially completed questionnaires:* They had to be discounted.

TABLE 3.5: Sample of student-population size for CT

School	Department	S1	S3	S4	R1	R3	R4
Engineering	Engineering I	150			121		
	Engineering III		50			78	
	Engineering IV			35			19
Marketing and management	Marketing I	150			107		
	Marketing III		75			24	
	Marketing IV			35			24
Life sciences	Environmental health I	55			35		
	Environmental health III		25			—	
	Environmental health IV			20			—
Design	Design I	55			100		
	Design III		25			—	
	Design IV			35			—
Education	Education I	50			44		
	Education III		25			18	
	Education IV			25			—
TOTAL		460	200	150	406	120	43

S1, 3, 4 = Selected sample size of student population for year group 1, 3, 4
R1, 3, 4 = Realised sample size of student population for year group 1, 3, 4

TABLE 3.6: Sample of student-population size for PT

Faculty	Department	S1	S3	S4	R1	R3	R4
Engineering	Engineering I	260			162		
	Engineering III		150			71	
	Engineering IV			40			7
Life sciences	Environmental health I	60			56		
	Environmental health III		40			20	
	Environmental health IV			50			60
Business sciences	Economics I	150			89		
	Marketing and management III		100			—	
	Economics IV			40			—
Art and design	Graphic design I	51			37		
	Graphic design III		30			—	
	Graphic design IV			20			—
Education	NDHDE I	50			49		
	NDHDE III		80			64	
	NDHDE IV						67
TOTAL		571	400	150	393	155	134

S1, 3, 4 = Selected sample size of student population for year group 1, 3, 4
R1, 3, 4 = Realised sample size of student population for year group 1, 3, 4

A profile of the sample[3]

The data set for the study comprises 5 629 students. Because one of the particular foci of the survey is that of institutional differences, the various distributions have been presented by institution. For each institution the research team identified a number of key variables which it considered to have a significant bearing on students' information-literacy abilities and needs. These are race, gender, language, year group, disciplinary domain and age.

Race

The graph below shows that the sample, to a large extent, reflects the existing racial distribution of students in the region. UWC and PT draw the highest number of black students with the three historically advantaged institutions (HAIs) drawing the greatest proportion of white students.

GRAPH 3.1: Analysis of student sample by race

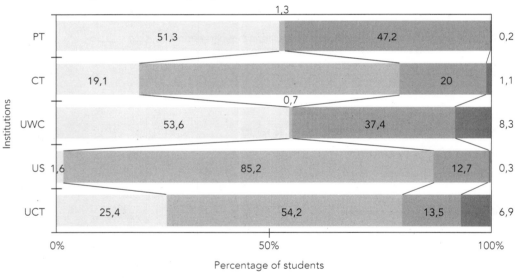

Geographical area

The graph below presents the demographic analysis of the sample. It is interesting to note that generally speaking US and CT can be regarded as provincial institutions drawing the majority (62,7% and 78,7% respectively) of their students from the Western Cape. UWC (51%) and UCT (47%) draw a significant number of students from other parts of the country. UCT is the institution which draws the greatest number of students from outside of South Africa (8%).

GRAPH 3.2: Analysis of student sample by geographical distribution

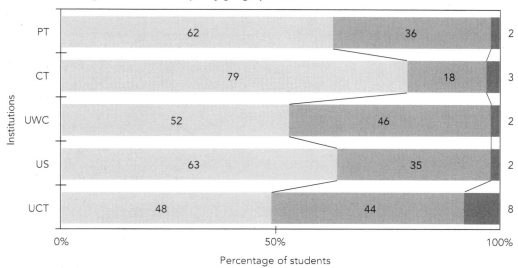

Language

GRAPH 3.3: Analysis of student sample by home language

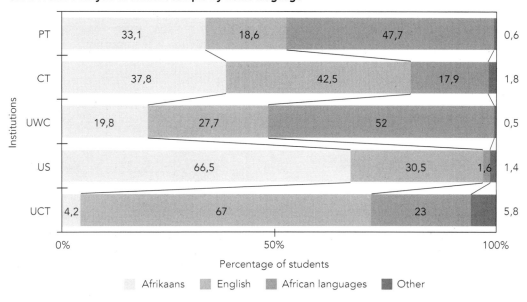

From the graph above it is clear that Afrikaans is the first language of most students at Stellenbosch (67%), English at UCT (67%), while some African language is the preferred language of a majority of students at UWC (52%). Interestingly there are small differences between the proportions of Afrikaans- (38%) and English-speaking students (43%) at CT, whereas speakers of African languages are in the largest proportion of all language groups (48%) at PT.

Gender

GRAPH 3.4: Analysis of student sample by gender

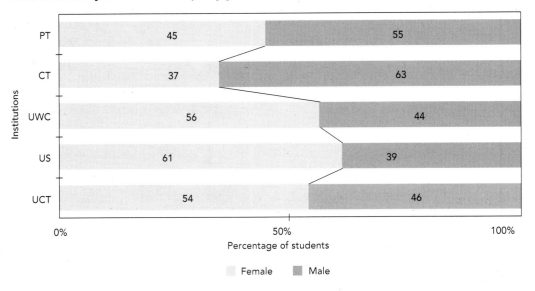

The overall gender breakdown is 53 per cent female and 47 per cent male. The biggest deviations from this picture are US (61:39), CT (37:63) and PT (45:55). Of the five institutions, US has the largest proportion of female students. It is important to note that the technikons report the lowest proportion of females students.

Age

GRAPH 3.5: Analysis of student sample by age

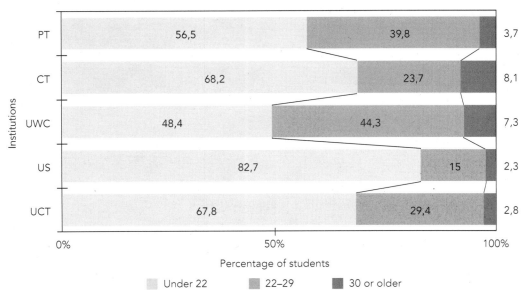

The overall distribution shows 66 per cent of the students to be under 22 years of age, 30 per cent between 22 and 29, and four per cent 30 years or older. The most significant feature of Graph 3.5 is the big difference between the profiles of PT and UWC on the one hand (both reveal more than 39% students in the age group 22 to 29) and US, CT and PT on the other. In both cases, further analysis reveals that the majority of students in this age group in these institutions are black students (65% of the students at UWC and 69% of the students at PT between 22 and 29 are black). The table also indicates that UCT has a significant component of students in the age category 22 to 29 (29%). Analysis reveals that whereas UWC students in this cohort are mainly undergraduates, UCT has mainly postgraduate students in this age category.

In general, the sample drawn for the survey is fairly representative of the distribution of students in the subjects chosen at the five higher-education institutions. This was confirmed in the focus-group interviews.

The profile of the sample described reflects the pattern of higher education that characterised apartheid education with CT, US and UCT attracting mainly white students. UWC and PT draw the majority of black students.

Performance

GRAPH 3.6: Analysis of student sample by reported performance scores

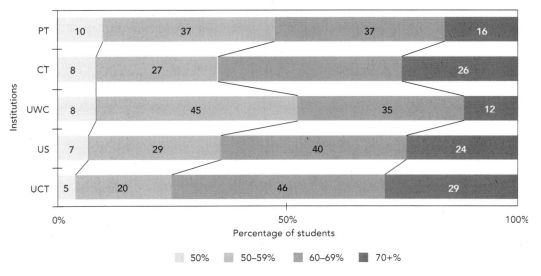

The graph above indicates that UWC and PT have the greatest proportion of students reporting performance scores in the ranges below 50 per cent and 50 to 59 per cent. At UCT, US and CT there are a high proportion of students reporting scores 70 per cent and above. It is interesting to note that at least a third of the sample report scores in the range 60 to 69 per cent.

Data collection

In order to accomplish the distribution of the requisite 6 000 questionnaires, eleven fieldworkers were recruited. A briefing session was held at which fieldworkers were introduced to the aims of the project and the procedures for collecting the data.

Four fieldworkers volunteered to take on the responsibility of co-ordinating the administration process at the institutions. This involved dealing with any problems regarding timetables, and included organising further visits where necessary. They were also responsible for overseeing the post-coding of the questionnaires. Fieldworkers were requested to provide a report upon completion of the administration of the questionnaires. After permission had been granted by the various ethics or research committees, deans and heads of department as well as lecturers were approached for their permission. Timetables were accordingly established for institutions and distributed to fieldworkers who had been provided with the required questionnaires. The fieldworkers were responsible for approaching the lecturer/s to introduce themselves and confirm that the initial arrangements were still suitable. Thereafter they approached the class, explained their presence and asked students to complete the questionnaire during class time.

Data analysis

Fieldworkers recorded the administration of the questionnaires and post-coded them. The post-coding was checked by fieldworkers who had volunteered to act as lead co-ordinators. Further coding of the open-ended questions (items 4.17, 4.30, 4.42, 5.11) was then undertaken. Minor errors were corrected and incomplete questionnaires discarded during this period.

During the post-coding and analysis stages certain changes were made to the data captured. The main changes involved recoding of variables. The main re-codings which were applied to the data set are discussed in subsequent sections.

Results in major subjects

The six-category classification as contained in the questionnaire (item 1.4) was re-coded to a four-category system by collapsing the first two and last two categories. The new variable (Perform) now consists of four categories and the results for the total data set are presented in chart 1.

Matric examination boards

In addition to the eight response options in the questionnaire, a further 30+ options were exercised by respondents. It was decided to create six main categories in the following way: The four "white" examination boards (Cape, Transvaal, Natal, Free State) were grouped together, as were the House of Representatives and House of Delegates examination boards, the Department of

CHART 3.1: Student performance by percentage in major subjects

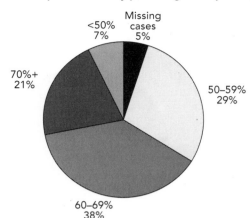

Education and Training and the Transkei-Bophuthatswana-Venda-Ciskei categories were retained as such, all overseas examination boards (e.g. Cambridge) were grouped together and, finally, the independent examination boards (Independent Examination Board/JMB) were grouped together. The results are summarised in Chart 3.2.

CHART 3.2: Analysis of sample according to matric examination boards

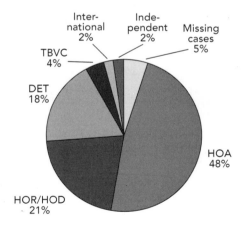

Language

The distribution of languages before being re-coded is presented in Chart 3.3a. It was decided to re-code home language because of the small cell values for some of the African languages as well as other European languages. The categories for Afrikaans and English were retained, while all African languages were grouped together, with the remainder allocated to a category "Other languages" (Chart 3.3b).

CHART 3.3a: First-language distribution of sample by percentage

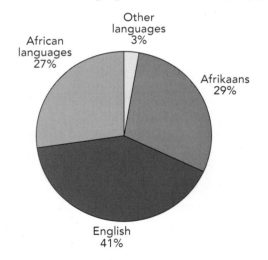

Zulu 2,4% Venda 0,3%
Xhosa 16,7%
Other languages 2,5%
Tswana 2,8%
Tsonga 0,6%
Swazi 0,6%
Southern Sotho 1,9%
Northern Sotho 1,2%
Ndebele 0,3%
Afrikaans 28,8%
English 40,5%

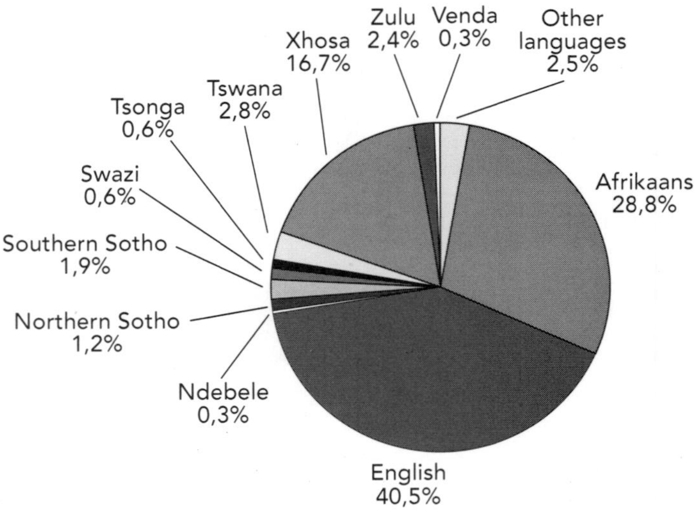

CHART 3b: Re-coded first-language distribution of sample by percentage

African languages 27%
Other languages 3%
Afrikaans 29%
English 41%

Geographical area

During the manual post-coding process, responses to item 2.3 ("Please name the TOWN in which you matriculated") had already been coded. Three categories were created: Western Cape, the rest of South Africa, outside South Africa. The distribution of responses is presented in Chart 3.4.

Subjects/disciplinary areas

The subjects that were surveyed for the study were re-coded into main disciplinary areas. Chart 3.5 presents the re-coded subjects.

CHART 3.4: Geographic distribution of the sample by percentage

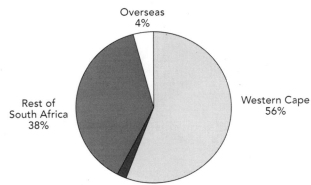

CHART 3.5: Distribution of disciplines in the sample by percentage

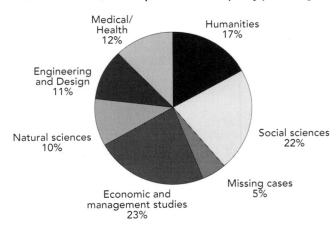

Subjects were re-coded into the above categories as follows:

■ English and law = arts and humanities
■ Psychology and education = social sciences
■ Economics, management sciences and accounting = economic and management sciences
■ Physics and chemistry = natural sciences
■ Civil and mechanical engineering/industrial, graphic and applied design/photography = engineering and design studies
■ Medicine, nursing science and environmental health = medical and health sciences

Year group

The year groups were divided as follows: Junior undergraduate (first-year students), senior undergraduate (third-year students) and postgraduate students. The results of the first re-coding are presented in chart 3.6.

CHART 3.6: Year-group distribution in the sample by percentage

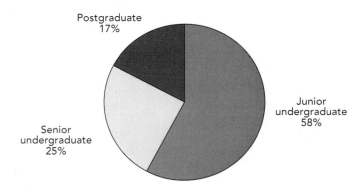

Process of analysis

The data was analysed using SPSS to

- determine the frequency counts for each item
- tabulate the frequency counts in relation to variables identified, namely race, gender, year level, subject and age
- determine and construct indexes using factor analysis for each of the main sections of the student questionnaires (sections 3, 4 and 5), and determine the predictor variables for each of the items

The results were compiled as three preliminary reports which constituted the basis of discussion with each of the five higher-education institutions. The first report presented a general global overview of the responses to each item. The second report provided a profile of each of the five institutions on the basis of six identified variables, namely year group, disciplinary domain, race, gender, language and academic performance, and row indexes, namely library usage and computer competence. The third report developed indexes for the items and ascertained the main predictor variables.[4]

Second focus-group interview concerning preliminary results

Following the preliminary results of the student questionnaires, open-ended focus-group interviews were held at the five institutions. The focus-group comprised the vice-rector (academic affairs), the heads/directors of the academic development centres/units, computer centres/services, information-technology divisions/units, library, the chairpersons of library committees and lecturers whose classes were surveyed. Persons identified as part of this group were requested to nominate alternates if they themselves were unable to attend.

The purpose of the focus-group interviews was to discuss the results obtained from the analysis of the student questionnaire. Participants were presented with the preliminary results beforehand. At the interview, participants were asked whether they believed that the results reflected the state of information literacy as they perceived it at their institution. They were also asked to provide possible explanations for the trends and patterns that were revealed through the analysis of the data.

The focus-group interviews were also important since they afforded the research team an opportunity to discuss the results with the institutions prior to the publication of the final book. In this respect, they created greater awareness of the issues raised in the study.

Issues of representativeness and generalisation

Concerns with the representativeness of the samples realised in the survey led to validation of the findings through comparison with institutional records, as well as the feedback and commentary obtained in the second round of institutional focus-group discussions. These efforts have been made to ensure that the findings could be generalised.

In order to ensure that the realised sample at each of the institutions reflected the global student profile, efforts were made to correlate the findings with institutional records. This did not prove possible in every instance due to the inaccessibility of these records. The records that were obtained showed that the retrieved sample proved an accurate reflection of the entire student population.

The second focus-group interviews also acted as a check on the findings. Care has been taken not to conflate discrepancies around interpretations of findings which are inevitable, with concerns regarding statistical or quantitative inaccuracies. Where conflicting interpretations have arisen, these discussions have also been reflected.

Limitations of the study

The main findings of the study were drawn from questionnaires administered to students. The questionnaires are self-reporting instruments which report on perceptions of individuals. Therefore, they do not always represent what actually happens. For example, the student questionnaire asked to report on students' academic performance in their courses. However, since these results were not checked against institutional figures, they may not necessarily be correct in each instance.

A further limitation of the study was that the research team was not able, due to time and resource constraints, to conduct in-depth interviews with students and academics regarding information-literacy practices. Such interviews would have yielded a richer and more textured picture of information-literacy needs and practices.

An additional constraint was the inability to achieve the desired sample in all cases. Specifically it was not possible, for reasons mentioned earlier, to realise adequate sample sizes for the first- and third-year undergraduate cohort. It is therefore difficult to draw firm conclusions regarding the state of information literacy across the year levels. However, Chi-Squared Automatic Interaction Detection (CHAID) analysis did not report year group as being an important predictor of information-literacy abilities and needs, though year groups emerged as being important in the analysis of results by indices (cf. Chapter 6).

This chapter has reported on the methods and procedures adopted in the investigation. Key issues and problems have been highlighted. The methodological discussions of the resource group suggested that an important follow-up to this study would be an in-depth investigation of specific programmes and projects that were consciously developing information-literacy education. This is a direction that the Infolit project is to pursue in future, with specific reference to the pilot projects that have been funded.

The next chapter reports on and discusses the main findings obtained from the student questionnaire regarding their information-literacy abilities and needs.

Notes

[1] See "Second focus-group interview concerning preliminary results and issues of representativeness and generalisability" in this chapter for a more detailed account of the focus-group interviews.

[2] All percentages have been rounded off to the nearest whole.

[3] A more detailed breakdown of the sample can be found in Chapter 4 which profiles each institution.

[4] These reports have been made available to the five institutions and can be obtained from the Infolit offices.

4

Overview of Information Literacy in the Western Cape Region – by Institution

Karin de Jager

This chapter provides a general overview of each of the five institutions that were surveyed. It provides a global profile of information literacy in the region based on responses to each of the items of the student questionnaire (see Appendix A). The discussion in this chapter is based on comparative tables of the total student responses to individual questions, as well as on individual frequency counts by selected variables for each institution. The comparative tables of total student responses are attached to the end of this chapter, while the frequency counts by selected variables for each institution are obtainable from each institution. This chapter first presents the profiles of the three universities, the University of Cape Town (UCT), the University of Stellenbosch (US) and the University of the Western Cape (UWC), and the two technikons Cape Technikon (CT) and Peninsula Technikon (PT) respectively, according to various aspects of information literacy as addressed in the questionnaire.

The questionnaire consists of five sections, requiring different types of responses, and a final section for open-ended, voluntary responses which will not be analysed in this chapter. Section 1 elicited demographic details regarding age, gender, race and self-reported academic achievement. Section 2 elicited information on informants' prior schooling and required the completion of details about the schools at which respondents matriculated. Responses to sections 1 and 2 were discussed in Chapter 3.

Section 3, questions 3.1 to 3.9, requested respondents to complete a five-point semantic differential rating scale indicating very positive, positive, neutral, negative and very negative responses. In analysing this section, both responses on each side of the mid-point were added together to indicate either a "positive" or a "negative" response in every case.

Section 4, questions 4.1 to 4.6 consisted of a three-point rating scale indicating whether students had experienced certain activities "often", "sometimes" or "never". In analysing this section, experiences recorded as "sometimes" occasionally were added to either the "often" or the "never" responses (as indicated in the text) to illustrate the total number of responses reporting a certain experience at least sometimes.

Questions 4.7 to 4.14 comprised a four-point rating scale and respondents were required to indicate (1) confidence in their ability to use computers or software, (2) some experience, but no confidence, (3) no experience, but the desire to learn, and (4) no experience and no need to learn. The responses in this section are discussed as they were received. Questions 4.15 to 4.20 required yes/no responses and 4.21 to 4.30 inquired about the frequency with which students engaged in certain activities on a four-point scale where (1) indicated once per week or more often, (2) once per month or more often, (3) once per semester or more often or (4) never or hardly ever. Questions 4.31 to 4.42 and section 5, questions 5.1 to 5.11, consisted of three-point rating scales as discussed under questions 4.1 to 4.6, and a similar method of analysis was employed in considering this data.

Throughout the discussion of all five institutional profiles, the total percentage of responses for different questions was noted, followed by a consideration of analyses of frequency counts by the selected variables which were most prominently represented in a given response. In all instances, questions that were chosen for discussion of a particular institution were those in which the results from that institution seemed in some way significant or distinguishable from the rest.

University of Cape Town

The sample at this institution comprised 1 747 responses with a proportion of 76 per cent undergraduate to 24 per cent postgraduate, in comparison to the 68:32 ratio of the entire university population. Of concern here is that it had not been possible to realise a postgraduate sample in certain areas, so that there are no students represented in that category in the natural sciences.

Section 1 of the questionnaire elicited the main demographic characteristics of the respondents from each institution. Answers to the first question on the questionnaire reveal that UCT students are mainly young (68% under 22 years of age), while only three per cent are older than 30. The female:male ratio is 54:46, which is almost identical to the sample for all five institutions together (53:47). Responses regarding racial classification indicate that 25 per cent of the sample classified themselves as African, 54 per cent as white, 14 per cent as coloured and seven per cent as Indian. The proportions for the sample as a whole were: 28 per cent African; 44 per cent white; 23 per cent coloured and four per cent Indian.

As far as the reported academic performance from UCT is concerned, the highest proportion of the sample (29%) reported high academic performance (obtaining more than 70%) in their major or intended major subjects during this year, while the smallest proportion (5%) reported that they had obtained less than 50 per cent (failing performance).

Section 3 of the questionnaire was designed to test the levels of confidence and motivation with which students engage in their information-seeking activities. Students' confidence seems to be expressed by preparedness to act as leaders of groups and by working alone, rather than by participating in classroom activities. The highest number of UCT respondents (42%) replied affirmatively when asked whether they like to act as the leader of a group when a task has been assigned.[1]

Respondents were much less positive about whether they like to answer lecturers' questions in class (18% replied affirmatively) or to speak up in class when opinions were asked (27% replied affirmatively). They also tend to be unwilling to ask questions in class (36% replied positively, which was the second-lowest response). When questioned whether respondents are keen to tackle a challenging assignment, 42 per cent agreed.[2]

When cross-tabulated with other variables, the responses in this section indicate that the most significant factor related to confidence and motivation at UCT is academic performance. When asked whether they like to act as the leader for a group when a task has been assigned or whether they are eager to tackle a challenging assignment, 54 and 53 per cent of respondents who also reported high academic performance, replied affirmatively.[3]

A question about whether they prefer to participate in informal study groups or to work on their own, shows that 55 per cent of all UCT respondents prefer to work on their own. A further question probing self-reliance versus reliance on group experience confirms this result, as 53 per cent indicate that they rely on their own, rather than on group experiences.[4] Further analysis of question 3.8 shows that the greatest preference for working alone comes from students in the humanities (49%), computer-competent students (41%), those that are Afrikaans-speaking (40%) and senior undergraduates (40%). Students speaking African languages (21%), frequent library users (14%) and those with low academic performance (14%) most favour group work.

In section 4 responses to the questions designed to measure aspects of academic literacy involving reading and writing, show that 77 per cent of UCT students reported that they find prescribed readings difficult to understand either often or sometimes.[5] Seventy-six per cent of students reported that they were given too many readings with which to cope, and 63 per cent reported at least some difficulty in expressing their own ideas.[6] Analysis of the UCT results shows that students who reported that they never had difficulties with understanding readings, are high academic performers or computer-competent (both 35%), or they

"Students' confidence seems to be expressed by preparedness to act as leaders of groups and by working alone, rather than by participating in classroom activities."

are white (30%). Students who said they were often given too many readings with which to cope, are those with low academic performance (46%), or speakers of African languages (35%), or studying in the domains of the social sciences and education (29%).

Students' computer literacy and their access to computers were tested in the questions that followed. UCT generally fared well in these sections, so that 37 per cent of UCT students could report that they are competent at using a computer-operating system such as DOS or Windows, and 47 per cent report competence at using a word-processing package. More than 30 per cent of respondents in both cases furthermore report some experience of an operating system and a word-processing package.[7] Competence figures decrease with the more specific computer applications such as spreadsheets (19% report competence/confidence), databases (10%), graphics programmes (11%), statistical analyses (5%) and computer-aided design (CAD) (6%), while the responses "unable to use but would like to" rise commensurately. At UCT, significantly more male than female students report competence with reference to the use of all the computer applications mentioned in this section of the questionnaire.[8]

The extent to which students have access to computers was probed next. At UCT, 78 per cent of respondents claim to have access to a computer for their own use, and of those who do, 49 per cent have access on campus. Further analysis reveals that students at UCT who have the most access to computers, are either in the economic and management sciences, or white (both 85%), or are infrequent library users (84%).[9] Students reporting no access to computers at UCT are African (34%) or not computer-competent (33%).

Internet use is not yet widespread among undergraduate students on all the campuses. At UCT, more than 50 per cent of students with high computer confidence (61%), or postgraduate students (51%), or students in the economic and management sciences (50%) have access to the Internet. Of those who do report Internet access, some 65% have access on campus and they use it mainly to obtain information.

"Internet use is not yet widespread among under-graduate students on all the campuses."

Questions 4.18 to 4.20 were intended to measure exposure to academic-development programmes and library-skills instruction. While most UCT students (72% of the sample) claim to have attended library-orientation sessions, only 27 per cent attended sessions on study skills and 19 per cent advanced library instruction. The students likeliest to have attended study-skills sessions are in the natural sciences (51%), or speakers of African languages (47%), or academic performers in the range 50 to 59 per cent (38%). It was however pointed out in the focus-group interviews that where study skills have been infused with academic programmes, students might not have regarded them as being separate courses and might therefore have answered in the negative.

The questions probing library literacy may fruitfully be read in conjunction with question 3.7, which asked whether students were sufficiently confident to approach a librarian for assistance. Answers show that UCT students (73%) are the most willing of all to approach a librarian, and at UCT too, the highest percentage of students (39%) claim to visit the library once per week or more often in order to use the short-loan collection. The open shelves are used to find relevant readings once per week or more often by 32 per cent. The most frequent users of the short-loan collection are students in the humanities (68%), or speakers of African languages (54%), while the main frequent users of the open shelves are students in social sciences and education (49%), students in the humanities (47%) and African students (41%).

Responses from UCT show that while only 22 per cent of students with academic scores below 50 per cent report frequent use of open-shelf material, 35 per cent of students reporting achievement of over 70 per cent claim to be frequent users of the open shelves. Of the students performing at the 50 to 59 per cent level, 32 per cent claim to be frequent open-shelf users, as do 30 per cent of those scoring 60 to 69 per cent. While there therefore seems to be some correlation between the use of open-shelf materials and academic performance at UCT, there is little correlation between the use of the reserve collection and academic performance.

The last 12 questions in section 4 consisted of an information-literacy needs assessment. The results suggested that UCT students in general are somewhat less "needy" than those at the other institutions, although students at all institutions seem to be expressing a need for more help than they are actually getting from their educational institutions. At UCT, 32 per cent of students say that they never need help with writing essays and the students in the least need such of assistance are high academic achievers (45%), or computer-competent (43%), or white (42%). Students with the lowest academic performance, or students speaking African languages, express the most need for help with writing and referencing, while the greatest need for computer training is expressed by those who regard themselves as not computer-competent. There seems to be very little gender difference in expressed need for assistance with writing, referencing and finding library materials, but more females than males declare a need for computer-skills training. The greatest need for Internet training is expressed by coloured students (59%) and those who regard themselves as not very computer-competent (55%).

The final section 5 was designed to obtain a reflection of the extent to which independent learning takes place (or is perhaps encouraged) at the five institutions. From the responses it becomes clear that at UCT traditional methods of learning and assessment are still prevalent. Activities such as the writing of essays and finding relevant readings without reading lists are common: 92 per cent of respondents wrote essays during the past six months, and

"... UCT students in general are somewhat less 'needy' [in terms of learner support] than those at the other institutions, although students at all institutions seem to be expressing a need for more help ..."

73 per cent found relevant readings on their own, while 25 per cent never did practical assignments. Media-based learning activities such as watching television, listening to the radio or reading newspapers to find information are not very prominent at UCT: 50 per cent of UCT students claim that they never looked at films or television for information during the past six months.[10] Working in small groups seems to be much more common (only 8% of UCT students never did this during the past six months) than making oral presentations (which 38 per cent never did) or doing fieldwork (which 54% never did in this period).

"The students [from US] who are least confident in answering questions, seem to be those who use the library infrequently ..."

University of Stellenbosch

The institutional sample at US consisted of 1 296 respondents in the proportion 85 per cent undergraduate to 15 per cent postgraduate, in comparison to the 70:30 ratio of the entire population at this institution. It did not prove possible to realise the desired postgraduate sample at this institution either, thus rendering it impossible to make detailed comparisons between postgraduate students in different faculties or across institutions.

Responses to section 1 from US indicate that this student body seems to be the youngest of all institutions, with 83 per cent of respondents younger than 22 years. The female to male ratio is 61:39, so that considerably more females were present in the US sample than in the total sample for all the institutions, which was 53:47. Focus-group interviewees reported a growing female student population and were not surprised by this figure. The racial composition of the sample was largely white (85%), with 13 per cent coloured, less than two per cent African and less than one per cent Indian.

Reported academic performance from US shows that 24 per cent of respondents claim to have achieved more than 70 per cent in their major or intended major subjects. Lowest academic performance is reported by seven per cent of the sample.[11]

The US responses to section 3 measured confidence and motivation indicate that students here also express their confidence by acting as leaders in class, by facing challenges and by working alone. A large proportion of US respondents (42%) are very willing to act as leaders of task groups[12] or to tackle challenging assignments (51%). They are, however, not prepared to answer lecturers' questions in class (15% answered positively). The students who are least confident in answering questions, seem to be those who use the library infrequently (57%), and more females (52%) than males (40%) say they never know what to say when lecturers ask questions. Focus-group interviewees suggested that the apparent unwillingness to participate in classroom activities could partly be ascribed to the generally more authoritarian Afrikaans culture at this institution. Students from US are the most eager from all surveyed to work alone (57%), whereas

24 per cent express preference for working in groups with their classmates.

The first six questions in section 4 were designed to test aspects of academic literacy, and while results from this investigation clearly show that students from all five institutions have difficulties in this area, indications are that US students also have less difficulties than the others. More students from this institution than any other claim never to have any difficulty structuring essays (37%), or with expressing other writers' ideas (33%), or with understanding readings (30%). Further analysis of US responses show that groups of students who claim to have the least difficulty in these areas, are students from the medical or health sciences in the first place (61% never have difficulties in understanding readings), or postgraduates (50% never have such difficulties). Students with the highest reported academic performance also consistently report fewer difficulties than the norm for all the questions in this section.

Responses to the questions designed to test aspects of respondents' computer literacy, show that 34 per cent of US students report competence or confidence in using computer-operating systems, while 32 per cent are competent in using word-processing software and 25 per cent are confidently able to use spreadsheets. Here, too, it is evident that competence decreases with the more specific computer applications such as databases (8% report the ability to use such a software package competently), graphics programmes (9%), statistical analysis (6%) and CAD (4%), while the responses "unable to use but would like to" rise commensurately. Analysis reveals that students in the economic and management sciences report more confidence in using the different computer applications than students in the other disciplinary domains.

Access to computers at US is reported by 73 per cent of respondents,[13] but computer provision on campus is highest at US where 71 per cent of students who use computers, do so on campus. Of the students reporting access to a computer at US, the largest proportion are from the natural sciences (85%), closely followed by students in the economic and management sciences (84%). Of all the institutions, the largest proportion US students use e-mail (37%),[14] and the largest proportion of the US students (85%) that use e-mail, do so on campus.[15] The highest proportion of students in the natural sciences (85%) and in the economic and management sciences, as well as those who were able to use computers (both 84%) have access to computers. Somewhat surprisingly, 38 per cent of postgraduate students report that they do not have access to computers,[16] while the lowest proportion of students who do not have access to computers are in the medical/health sciences. It was reported in the focus-group discussion that US has embarked on a programme to provide both access and training in new forms of technology so that these results were perceived as reflective of the institutional drive towards greater computer literacy and usage.

"... it is evident that competence decreases with the more specific computer applications, such as databases, graphics programmes, statistical analysis and CAD, while the responses 'unable to use but would like to' rise commensurately."

Students at US who have access to the Internet are from the natural sciences (51%), or computer-competent (48%), or frequent library users (40%). They mostly use the Internet to obtain information or to make contact with others.

In the next series of questions, the percentage of US students reporting to have attended study-skills programmes (20%), or advanced library instruction (12%), is the smallest of all the institutions. Even though basic library orientation is least well established at US, 61% of students claim to have attended sessions, suggesting good library penetration at all five institutions.

Students who frequently attended study-skills programmes at US are African (45%) or coloured (28%), or doing social sciences and education (31%). Those who attended advanced library-instruction sessions, are frequent library users in any case. This situation was acknowledged in the focus-group interviews. It was emphasised that the institution was embarking on a programme to widen the coverage of the academic-development and library programmes. It was also pointed out that low library instruction could possibly be related to the fact that the institution has a multi-media library-training programme which students can access at any time and independently.

"It was suggested in the focus group that the teacher-centred approach to instruction, which is still prominent at the institution, could discourage independent learning."

The following ten questions dealt with aspects of library literacy, and results show that US students use the open shelves far less than the other institutions.[17] Only 13 per cent of US students use open shelves once a week or more often.[18] The reasons for this apparently low usage may be quite complex, as US students are, after UCT, the most likely to approach librarians for assistance (question 3.7). It was suggested in the focus group that US students could possibly obtain all the material they require from their own text books or the reserve collection, while it could be that students at the historically disadvantaged institutions (HDIs) may turn to the open shelves in response to the inadequacy of their short-loan collections. Focus-group discussions also suggested that a further factor could be the strong course-reader culture at US.

US students also seem least inclined of all the respondents to use abstracts and indexes, to look for other readings from references in articles that they have read, or to find relevant material that has not specifically been prescribed; all indicating either that their information needs have been met, or that they are not encouraged to search for information on their own. It was suggested in the focus group that the teacher-centred approach to instruction, which is still prominent at the institution, could discourage independent learning. Students who never use abstracts, indexes or bibliographies, are the infrequent library users (72%), or students in the natural sciences (51%). These are also the students who never look for other readings from references, although 53 per cent of the highest academic performers never look for extra readings either.

Students likeliest to use the open shelves once a week or more often, are the frequent library users (52%), or senior undergraduate and postgraduate students (both 22%). There seems to be no relationship between open-shelf library use and reported academic performance at US, as 12 per cent of the high academic performers report that they use the open shelves once a week or more often, while 11 per cent of those that report failing grades do the same. These observations might tend to support the suggestion that independent library use is not encouraged at US.

The focus group pointed out that this situation was perhaps due to heavy reliance on one or two prescribed texts and the fact that lecture notes were issued in every class, making library usage less important. In general, it was reported that there was a heavy reliance on the lecture and lecturer with minimal attempt to get students to seek independent readings. One focus-group respondent claimed that there was "too much spoon-feeding" at this institution. It was also suggested that low library usage could reflect the capacity of students to purchase the prescribed texts, thus making library work unnecessary.

From the section aiming to address issues of need, it appears that US students seem to be somewhat less in need of help with information-literacy skills such as writing essays, understanding references and compiling them and also with finding library materials, than students from the other institutions. US respondents who need most help with writing essays study the humanities (21% need help "often"), or are African (20%). Infrequent library users (50%) never have any difficulty finding things in the library.

As far as computer-skills training is concerned, US respondents tend to be grouped among those in less need of training than those at the other institutions. The most need for different aspects of computer-skills training is expressed by students in the humanities and by those who regard themselves as not very computer-competent. While females need slightly more help with writing essays (16% said they "often" needed help vs 13% of males), they seem to need significantly more help with computer applications: 40 per cent often need help with training in word-processing *vs* 24 per cent males; 38 per cent often need help with spreadsheets *vs* 27 per cent males. The most need for Internet training is recorded by humanities students (56%) and those that do not regard themselves as computer-competent (52%).

The final section 5 of the questionnaire, which was designed to assess the extent to which independent learning takes place at the five institutions, indicates that at US activities such as writing essays, which 27 per cent of respondents have never done during the previous six months, and doing fieldwork, for which 62 per cent reported "never", takes place considerably less than at the other two universities. US respondents, however, report doing more practical assignments and they look at more films or videos than the other universities. Half of US students never made any oral presentations and nearly half (46%) never interviewed other people

"It was … suggested that low library usage could reflect the capacity of students to purchase the prescribed texts, thus making library work unnecessary."

for information during the past six months. They are also least likely of all students to find relevant readings without the help of reading lists (42% reported "never"), apparently confirming that techniques for fostering independent learning are not well established on this campus. Focus-group discussions also suggested that these findings perhaps had to do with Afrikaner culture which according to one respondent did not encourage independent and critical work.

University of the Western Cape

The institutional sample at UWC consisted of 1 270 responses in the proportion undergraduate to postgraduate of 83:17, which was the same for the population as a whole. It had not been possible to obtain a postgraduate sample in the natural sciences and, as stated before, detailed comparisons between postgraduate students in different faculties or across institutions were not possible.

As far as the reported academic performance from UWC is concerned, the most respondents (45% of the UWC sample) claim that they had obtained between 50 and 59 per cent in their major or intended major subjects during this year, while the smallest proportion (8%) reported obtaining less than 50 per cent. At UWC the smallest percentage at all the institutions (12%) reported achieving over 70 per cent, and 35 per cent reported achieving 60 to 69 per cent.

From section 3 of the questionnaire, which attempted to address issues of confidence and motivation, it seems that students from UWC are less confident in activities such as acting as the leader of a group (33% of UWC students replied positively[19]), and that they express confidence by participating actively in class. Thus they are motivated to answer lecturers' questions in class (27% replied positively, which was the second-highest response) and to speak up in class when opinions are asked (30% answered in the affirmative). The most confident students tend to be academic achievers obtaining over 70 per cent, or computer-competent, or from the medical and health sciences. Males also seem to be significantly more confident than females in response to all the questions in this section.

In the focus-group discussions, UWC students' confidence in participating in classroom activities was partly ascribed to the experience of student organisation and activism. However, not all focus-group respondents agreed that UWC students were active in lectures and tutorials. UWC students seem least eager of all to tackle a challenging assignment (39% answered positively).[20]

Although 44 per cent of all UWC respondents prefer to work alone rather than in groups (37%), more students speaking African languages (27%) prefer to work in groups than to work alone (23%).

As noted before, responses to the questions in section 4, which was designed to measure aspects of academic literacy, cause concern as they show that 88 per cent of UWC students find pre-scribed readings difficult to understand at least some of the time. More respondents from UWC (86%) than from any of the other institutions also complain that they are given too many readings at least some of the time (28% say "often") and 17 per cent often find it difficult to structure an essay. UWC respondents are least confi-dent about expressing their own ideas (a total of 70% reported dif-ficulties often or sometimes), or expressing those of other writers in their own words (80% reported difficulties). Predictably, the weakest academic performers are the least confident about expressing both their own and other writers' ideas. Infrequent library users report severe difficulties in these areas as well.

From the section dealing with computer competence and access, it is evident that a serious need for both skills and resources is expressed by students from UWC, who not only con-sistently report the least computer-competence of the five institu-tions, but also the most need for skills in the use of common soft-ware and applications such as operating systems, word-processing and spreadsheets. They also report the least skill in the use of com-puter-aided design programmes and multimedia. As at the other universities, more males than females report computer compe-tence, but there is no gender difference in reported access to com-puters.

Not unexpectedly, findings of low computer-competence go together with reports of the lowest access to computers at UWC. This is the only institution where fewer than half the respondents (44%) report that they have access to a computer for their own use.[21] Of the 44 per cent students at UWC who have access to computers, 62 per cent claim that this access is provided on campus, but it is clear that e-mail is not well-established among UWC students, as only seven per cent use it.[22]

UWC has recognised that the improvement of computer liter-acy and access has to be a priority at this institution. It was explained in the focus-group discussion that UWC has set itself the goal that all first-year students should be computer literate by the year 2000 and intends to achieve this by the extensive use of walk-in computer laboratories and the more effective deployment of existing resources.

Responses to the question whether students have attended a course on study skills, show the considerable extent to which academic-development programmes have penetrated the student body at UWC, where 31 per cent responded in the affirmative.[23] Students most likely to have attended a course in study skills are either computer-competent (44%), frequent library users (43%) or African (40%). This was ascribed to the well-developed academic-development programme that exists at the institution. Responses also indicate a strong library awareness, as 70 per cent attended a library-orientation session, and 21 per cent attended advanced library instruction.[24] Answers to the questions around library

"Predictably, the weakest academic performers are the least confident about expressing both their own and other writers' ideas. Infrequent library users report severe difficulties in these areas as well."

literacy indicate that UWC students use their reserve collection somewhat less than the other two universities. Open-shelf use seems unexpectedly high, as 42 per cent report that they used open shelves once a week or more often; also that 24 per cent looked for other readings from references in articles. The significance of these observations is somewhat unclear, as it has also been suggested that high reported usage of open-shelf material may be the result of poor stock and materials provision in both the reserve collection and the open shelves. In addition, the question of correlation between open-shelf use and academic performance seems inconclusive, as more students reporting achievement between 60 and 69 per cent use the open shelves (45%), than those reporting over 70 per cent (38%) or those achieving 59 per cent or less (41%).

Usage of computerised catalogues is considerably higher than that of card catalogues (36% *vs* 13%). It is believed that since card catalogues have not been available at the UWC library for some years, reports of card-catalogue use could possibly be explained by the many open-ended responses from students that, in addition to their own library, they also used public and other academic libraries in the region where card catalogues are still present.

Assistance by librarians is used by 53 per cent of respondents who report that they ask a librarian for help at least once a month or more often. One focus-group informant found this surprising as subject librarians are "tucked away" and not easily accessible to students. This observation is perhaps confirmed by the finding from question 3.7 that respondents from UWC (24%) report reluctance to ask a librarian for assistance. Responses also make it clear that students at UWC[25] are more inclined to look for, find and use non-prescribed material, but it is not clear whether this is in response to problems of availability of library materials or a result of methods of teaching and learning.

Responses to questions in the section dealing with needs analysis indicate that UWC is in many respects the "neediest" of the five institutions, with the highest percentage of "need help often"-responses for the questions concerning issues of both academic literacy and basic computer literacy. Of the entire sample, a large number of students from UWC say they often need help with writing essays (29%), with understanding and compiling references (24% and 22%), with finding things in the library (29%) and with training in word-processing, spreadsheets and databases. Most need for help with writing essays at UWC was expressed by students with the lowest academic performance (37%) and by students of the humanities (33%).

Students expressing high need for basic computer skills do not reflect significant gender differences.[26] A high need for Internet training is expressed by students in the medical/health sciences (66%) and by postgraduates (64%). These responses endorse the lack of an information-technology culture at UWC.

The final section 5 of the questionnaire shows that UWC

students in general are highly likely to have written essays during the past six months (66% reported "often"), but with US students the least likely to have worked in small groups (51% said "often", 9% said "never", in both cases).[27] They were also the least likely of all the respondents to have done practical assignments (only 42% said "often"). Thirty-six per cent of the proportion of students reported that they often watched television and listened to the radio, and 42 per cent reported that they read newspapers for information.[28] It is not clear whether this behaviour is encouraged or rewarded by lecturers, or whether it might be culturally or politically rooted.

Cape Technikon

The samples from the technikons were considerably smaller than from the universities, and that from CT was the smallest of all, consisting of 624 responses with 84 per cent from students in their first three years and 16 per cent in their fourth year. At the institution as a whole, this proportion is 87:13. As the numbers of fourth-year students are small, samples in this cohort were only obtained from students studying the domains of humanities/social sciences, management studies and engineering/design studies.

"... CT ... students tend to regard themselves as neither particularly confident, nor exceptionally hesitant."

Analysis of section 1 shows that respondents from this institution are mainly young (68% under 22 years of age) while eight per cent are older than 30, which is the highest proportion of all the institutions. There are considerably more males (63%) than females (37%) at CT. The racial composition of the sample was primarily white (60%), with 20 per cent coloured, 19 per cent African and one per cent Indian.

As far as the reported academic performance from the CT sample is concerned, the highest proportion of students (39%) said they obtained between 60 and 69 per cent in their major or intended major subjects during this year, while the smallest proportion (8%) reported that they had obtained less than 50 per cent. Almost equal proportions of students (26% and 27% respectively) reported that they had either achieved over 70 per cent, or between 50 and 59 per cent.

The responses from CT in section 3 seem to indicate that students tend to regard themselves as neither particularly confident, nor exceptionally hesitant. They are therefore to some extent prepared to act as leaders in groups (38% answered positively)[29] or to answer lecturers' questions in class (26%). They also are fairly likely to ask questions in class (47% replied positively)[30] and the likeliest of all to ask lecturers questions after class (56% said they like to speak to lecturers). They are, however, less willing to ask librarians for assistance (61% are prepared to approach a librarian; the second lowest response).[31] Students from CT most likely to approach a lecturer after class, are the frequent library users (64%) or the high achievers (61%), while those least likely to request help from librarians, are computer-competent or African. African students are also the most eager to ask questions in class (54% responded positively).

While it has become clear from all the responses to the first part of section 4 that students from all five institutions have difficulty with aspects of academic literacy involving reading and writing, it seems that CT students do not have as much difficulty as reported by the others.[32] The highest number of respondents from CT (40%) think they are never given too many readings, and 41 per cent never have any difficulty in expressing their own ideas. English-speaking (52%) or white (51%) students are never given too many readings, while students speaking African languages (49%) or high achievers (48%) never have difficulty in expressing their own ideas.

CT responses to questions designed to test computer literacy and access to computers generally indicate that these students are the most computer literate of all in the sample. The highest number of CT students report competence in using a word-processing package (55%), a computer-operating system (45%) or a spreadsheet package (30%). The most students from CT also report competence in more specific software applications such as graphics (15%), CAD (15%) and multimedia (19%). It is argued that the applied and practical nature of technikon courses could require that more students gain familiarity with these applications.

Reported access to computers is also the highest from CT, where 79 per cent of respondents have access to computers and 36 per cent use e-mail.[33] Students that are highly likely to have access to computers are computer-competent, senior undergraduates or in the economic and management sciences (90% in all three cases). Only 46 per cent of students who have access to computers, however, report that this access is available on campus. Students speaking African languages are likeliest to have access to computers on campus (75%) rather than at home.

The positive computer-access and literacy figures confirmed for the focus-group respondents the institution's emphasis on basic IT literacy. It was reported that most schools at the institution provided computer access, training and support. This was encouraged by CT through, for example, establishing 24-hour computer rooms.

In the section dealing with academic development and library skills, students from CT report relatively low attendance at courses on study skills, library orientation or advanced library-instruction sessions.[34]

African students in the sample from CT (54%) were the likeliest to have attended courses on study skills, while students in the social sciences and education were likeliest to have attended both library orientation (87%) and advanced library-instruction (34%) sessions.

The section designed to illuminate aspects of library literacy at the five institutions, show that CT students make the least use of

"CT responses to questions designed to test computer literacy and access to computers generally indicate that these students are the most computer literate of all in the sample."

their reserve collection (52% of respondents use the reserve collection once a semester or less often). Their use of the open-shelf collection is not exceptional (69% report use once a month or more often),[35] nor is their use of abstracts, indexes and bibliographies. They tend not to look for other readings either. The open shelves are used once a week or more often by 73 per cent of frequent library users, by 55 per cent of students in the economic and management sciences, and by 52 per cent of African students. There seems to be no relationship between open-shelf use and academic performance.

A large number of CT students (25%) have never asked a librarian for help, a finding that confirms the response to question 3.7 which also indicates some reluctance to approach librarians for assistance. It is not clear whether the apparently low use of library resources at this institution could be because library use is not encouraged or rewarded, or because of other reasons.

The section dealing with needs assessment shows that students at CT appear to be somewhat less in need of help with information-literacy skills such as writing essays, understanding and compiling references, and finding library materials than students from some of the other institutions.[36] Students who never need help with writing essays are in the medical/health sciences (51%), high academic achievers or infrequent library users (both 44%).

"The greatest need for Internet training is expressed by students in the economic and management sciences, by females or frequent library users."

As far as computer-skills training is concerned, CT students of all the respondents seem least in need of training with regard to word-processing and spreadsheets and tend to group themselves among those in less need of training in the more specialised applications. Students in the medical/health sciences, in the economic and management sciences and African students express the most need for basic computer-skills training such as word-processing and spreadsheets. Females seem to need more help "often" than males in everything except compiling references, finding things in the library and training in statistical-analysis programmes. The greatest need for Internet training is expressed by students in the economic and management sciences (66%), by females or frequent library users (both 58%).

Responses to the final section 5, dealing with learning styles and independent learning, do not produce clear differentiation between learning at the universities on the one hand and the technikons on the other. Instead, responses from CT cluster with those of US regarding the writing of essays,[37] which happens less at these two institutions than the others, or watching films or videos, which takes place more at US and CT than the others.[38] As far as other activities are concerned, such as working in small groups, doing field work or making oral presentations, the two technikons do seem to cluster together, and students engage in these activities somewhat more than students from the universities. CT students do more practical assignments (71% said "often") than any of the others. The increase in group-work confirmed, for the focus-group respondents, the growing institutional shift towards peer learning.

Peninsula Technikon

As noted above, the samples from the technikons were considerably smaller than those from the universities. The PT sample consisted of 687 responses, in the proportion 89 per cent first years to 11 per cent fourth years. As the numbers of fourth-year students are small, samples in this cohort were only obtained from students studying the two domains of humanities/social sciences and engineering/design studies.

Responses from this institution show that, while students here are mainly young (57% under 22 years of age), the middle age group (22 to 29 years of age) is larger (40%) than at any of the other institutions apart from UWC. There are more males (55%) than females (45%) at PT.[39] The racial composition of the sample was 51 per cent African, with 47 per cent coloured, one per cent white and less than one per cent Indian.[40]

The reported academic performance from the PT sample shows that equal proportions of students (37% in both cases) claim that they obtained between 60 and 69 per cent, or between 50 and 59 per cent in their major or intended major subjects during the year. Students reporting high academic achievement (over 70%) comprised 16 per cent of the sample, while 10 per cent report that they obtained less than 50 per cent.

"Of all the respondents, those from PT are the only ones who are equally as prepared to work alone as they are to work in groups with their classmates."

Responses to section 3 of the questionnaire indicate that students from PT tend to be more confident than other students in classroom activities such as answering lecturers' questions in class (34% replied positively), speaking up in class when opinions are asked (40% positive response) or asking questions in class (49% responded positively). They are, however, the least confident in acting as leaders in groups and not particularly eager to tackle challenging assignments. In the focus-group meeting, their apparent eagerness to participate in class was explained as a consequence of the pedagogical style which respondents felt to "be more engaging" at this institution. It was emphasised that PT encourages "interaction". However, this result was also met with some surprise, given that there is no developed tutorial programme at the institution.

The most confident students tend to be academic achievers obtaining over 70 per cent. African students also report being very ready to speak up or ask questions in class, while males seem to be more confident than females for most of the questions in this section. Of all the respondents, those from PT are the only ones who are equally as prepared to work alone as they are to work in groups with their classmates. English-speaking or coloured students prefer to work alone, while students speaking African languages prefer to work in groups.

It has been noted that section 4 was designed to measure aspects of academic literacy and seems to show that more than 70 per cent of students at all five institutions report that prescribed readings are difficult to understand at least some of the time. Of all the institutions, this figure is highest at PT where 89 per cent of respondents find prescribed readings difficult to understand at least sometimes. They also experience the most difficulties with expressing other writers' ideas and have the most difficulties in structuring an essay. PT students also claim to be among the least confident of expressing their own ideas. Students who have the most difficulty in expressing other writers' ideas, were the computer-incompetent or those with failing academic performance.

As far as the levels of computer literacy at PT are concerned, it is clear that a definite need for both skills and resources was expressed by students, who fairly consistently report low computer competence, as well as high needs for skills in the use of common software and applications such as operating systems and spreadsheets. As far as word-processing is concerned, however, they seem to be considerably more competent (44% claim competence).[41] They have had little exposure to multimedia (only 8% report competence),[42] but after CT have the most experience with CAD, which might be related to the nature of the courses at the technikons.

Student access to computers at PT is relatively poor (57% reported access).[43] The three HAIs report access of over 70 per cent. Of the students at PT that have access to computers, 71 per cent claim that this access is provided on campus, but the use of e-mail and the Internet on this campus is the lowest of all institutions. It was reported at the focus-group interview that there is minimal e-mail access for students at the undergraduate level at PT. It was also acknowledged that computer access was a problem that was being attended to, but that students did not have much access to computers at present and consequently computer-literacy levels were low.

The following three questions were intended to measure exposure to academic-development programmes and library-skills instruction. Responses to the question whether students have attended a course on study skills show that academic-development programmes have impacted on the student body at PT where 32 per cent replied in the affirmative.[44] Students at PT who are most likely to have attended a course in study skills, are either computer-competent (46%) or African (43%).

PT students are not particularly likely to have attended library-orientation sessions, but the most likely of all (24%) to have attended advanced library instruction. Students who attended advanced library-instruction sessions, were in their fourth year of study (45%), or in the social sciences and education (40%).

Responses to questions around library literacy suggest that 19 per cent of PT students never use their reserve collection, but PT

"Of the students at PT that have access to computers, 71 per cent claim that this access is provided on campus, but the use of e-mail and the Internet on this campus is the lowest of all institutions."

students use their open shelves more than any of the others, as 55 per cent report that they use open shelves once a week or more often. The significance of these observations is somewhat unclear, as it is possible that high reported usage of open-shelf material may be the result of poor stock and materials provision in both the reserve collection and the open shelves.[45]

In addition, some correlation between open-shelf use and academic performance seems apparent, as the most students reporting highest achievement (59%) use the open shelves once a week or more often, while 51 per cent of the frequent open-shelf users report failing academic achievement. It is not readily apparent why the fewest (49%), with grades between 60 and 69 per cent, report that they use the open shelves once a week or more often. The apparent relationship becomes somewhat more evident when it is noted that the fewest high achievers (10%) use the library only once a semester or never, that 15 per cent of those achieving 60 to 69 per cent; 16 per cent of those achieving 50 to 59 per cent and 20 per cent of those failing, use the library as infrequently as once a semester or never. It is, however, recognised that the relationship may be tenuous as the differences are not large.

The use of card catalogues was highest at PT (17%), which might be explained by the fact that the computer catalogue is still relatively new at this institution. PT students also seem to be well-established users of computer catalogues, as 39 per cent claim to use it once a week or more often.[46] The use of databases on CD-ROM (Compact-Disk Read Only Memory) is generally low at all the institutions, but the highest number of respondents who claim to use them once a week or more often, are from PT (8%).

It seems as if assistance by librarians is used and valued, as 35 per cent of PT students report that they ask a librarian for help at least once a week or more often. This was the highest response of all the institutions and is confirmed by PT responses to question 3.7, where 47 per cent indicated that they are prepared to ask a librarian for assistance. It is also evident that students at PT are most inclined to find and use non-prescribed material, but it is not clear whether this is in response to problems of availability of library materials or a result of methods of teaching and learning.

The last 12 questions in section 4 consisted of an information-literacy-needs assessment and responses tend to indicate that students from PT are in many respects the second-"neediest" of those at the five institutions.[47] Many students from PT often need help with writing essays (21%), with understanding references (20%) and compiling them (19%). Students who often need help with writing essays, study in the economic and management sciences (36%) or, perhaps unexpectedly, are the high academic achievers (30%).

PT students are also in greatest need of basic computer-skills training, such as in word-processing (42% "often" needed training), spreadsheets (42%) and database programmes (44%).[48] PT respondents express the greatest need of all for training in graphics programmes (45%), statistical analysis (41%), CAD (48%) and the Internet (57%). Their great need for Internet training is reinforced by responses indicating that Internet access on this campus is very low, which in turn suggests that issues of access and training should be addressed together. As far as training needs are concerned, gender differences do not seem pronounced, apart from the more specialised computer applications, where more males than females express serious need. Engineering and design students express the greatest need for Internet training (66%).

As was noted in the section dealing with CT, responses to the final section 5 of the questionnaire did not produce clear differentiation between learning at the universities on the one hand and the technikons on the other. In some respects, responses from PT resemble those of UWC, so that similar percentages report having done field work "often" (22% at PT, 20% at UWC), interviewed people (23% at both institutions) or watched television or listened to the radio for information (36% in both cases) during the past six months. As far as other activities are concerned, such as working in small groups, doing field work or making oral presentations, the two technikons seem to cluster together and engage in these activities somewhat more than students from the universities. PT students read newspapers for information more often and more consistently than any of the others: 91 per cent of respondents replied positively.

Conclusion

This chapter has highlighted and discussed key global features of students' information-literacy abilities and needs at the five higher-education institutions in the Western Cape region. While the chapter has focused on individual institutions, some reference was made to relevant comparison across them. Furthermore, the Chi-Test for independence was run on the tables presented below and it indicated that differences between institutions on all questions are statistically significant (p = 0,01). Thus, the differences in information-literacy abilities and needs discussed in this chapter are highly significant and reflect the institutional differences that exist in the region. This is also confirmed in the discussion in Chapter 5.

The next chapter focuses on students' information abilities and needs and provides a more detailed account of the overview presented here. Specifically Chapter 5 considers the various dimensions of students' information-literacy abilities and needs.

"As was noted in the section dealing with CT, responses to the final section 5 of the questionnaire did not produce clear differentiation between learning at the universities on the one hand and the technikons on the other."

Notes

[1] At UCT, 42 per cent of respondents also replied affirmatively; this was the highest response.
[2] The highest positive response was from US at 51 per cent; the lowest from UWC: 39 per cent.

3   It is interesting to note that the general trend of responses in this section seems to indicate that in some respects, UCT students are not quite as confident as those from PT and UWC, where students are clearly more eager to answer questions in class or to speak up when opinions are asked. It is suggested that this may be due to the history of organisational participation by students at the historically disadvantaged institutions. Students at the technikons seem most eager to ask questions in class, while UCT students prefer to act as leaders in groups.

4   In general, the results indicate that most students at all five institutions tend to prefer to work alone and be self-reliant rather than be part of a group.

5   It is sobering to note that more than 70 per cent of students at all five institutions report that they find prescribed readings difficult to understand at least some of the time.

6   At all the institutions more students said that they had difficulties in expressing another writer's ideas in their own words, than they said they had in expressing their own ideas.

7   Only CT reported even higher figures, but here the sample was very much smaller.

8   This trend is common across the region.

9   Among the students reporting access to computers, UCT is highest among the three universities (78%) and once more only bettered by CT (79%).

10   Activities such as watching television or listening to the radio (question 5.9), or reading newspapers to find information (question 5.10) are very popular at UWC and PT.

11   This pattern is very similar to that of both UCT and CT, although UCT reported slightly more students in the achievement range above 70 per cent (29% at UCT *vs* 24% at US) and fewer in the range 50 to 59 per cent (5% *vs* 7%).

12   Equal numbers of respondents from UCT and US answered affirmatively.

13   Access to computers at US was less than at both CT (79%) and UCT (78%).

14   Compared to 33 per cent at UCT.

15   Compared to 72 per cent at UCT.

16   Compared to 20 per cent at UCT.

17   The use of the short-loan or reserve collections on the other hand is comparable at the three universities: 39 per cent at UCT, 36 per cent at US and 34 per cent at UWC claim to use the reserve collection once a week or more often.

18   Compared to 42 per cent of UWC students and 32 per cent of UCT students who use open shelves once a week or more often.

19   Compared to 42 per cent from UCT and US, and 32 per cent from PT, which was the lowest.

20   The most eager respondents were from US (51 per cent).

21   The second lowest was from PT (57%), and the highest reported access (79%) was from CT.

22   Only PT had a comparably low figure of e-mail use (6%); the other four institutions reported more than 30 per cent use of e-mail by students.

23   At PT the figure was 32 per cent.

24   For both these questions, the UWC response was the second-highest of the five institutions.

25 Also at PT.
26 Only PT registered somewhat higher levels of need than UWC for more specialised computer-software training such as graphics programmes, statistical analysis, CAD and the Internet.
27 For both these questions the US result is the same as that of UWC.
28 These findings are similar at PT.
29 The highest was UCT at 42 per cent; the lowest PT at 32 per cent.
30 The highest was PT at 49 per cent.
31 The lowest positive response was 57 per cent at UWC.
32 Only US students report fewer difficulties than those from CT.
33 This is bettered only marginally by US, where 37 per cent e-mail use was reported.
34 Only US reported lower or the same low level of attendance.
35 Compared to 45 per cent at US and 86 per cent at PT.
36 Not surprisingly, students at UWC and PT report the highest levels of need.
37 37 per cent at CT and 42 per cent at US replied "often".
38 28 per cent at US and 29 per cent at CT "often" looked at films or videos for information during the past six months.
39 CT also has more males than females.
40 The proportions at UWC, which was the most comparable to PT, were: 54 per cent African, 37 per cent coloured, eight per cent Indian and one per cent white.
41 This figure is bettered only by CT (55%) and UCT (47%).
42 Only UWC students have had less: Six per cent report competence.
43 UWC was the only institution where fewer than half the respondents (44%) reported that they have access to a computer for their own use.
44 At UWC, 31 per cent.
45 This may also be the case at UWC.
46 This figure was only bettered by UCT.
47 After UWC.
48 Only UWC students express more need in these areas.

5

Students' Information-Literacy – Abilities and Needs

The data analysis involved a principal component analysis (using varimax rotation) of the main substantive items and the generation of six main indexes of the items in the questionnaire. Indexes are simply the clustering of cognate items based upon an analysis of the responses. The construction of each index is explained more fully below. The generation of indexes assists in identifying the key dimensions of information literacy from the responses to the questionnaire.

The factor analysis resulted in the following indexes, each of which is discussed below.

- Index of confidence
- Index of reading/writing ability
- Index of computer competence
- Index of library usage
- Index of information needs, including
  - Index of basic information needs
  - Index of computer-related needs
  - Index of advanced computer-related needs
- Index of independent learning, including
  - Index of interactive learning
  - Index of individual learning
  - Index of media-based learning

This chapter discusses each of the indexes in turn, providing an explanation for their construction. Each index is discussed firstly in terms of global institutional features, secondly in terms of patterns emerging in the total regional sample according to the variables, and thirdly by institution in relation to the variables. The six indexes below confirm many of the results reported in the preceding chapter but provide a more detailed breakdown of the responses using the key variables identified in the research, namely year group, disciplinary domain, academic performance, race, gender, language and age.

Index of confidence

The index of confidence is based on nine questions (questions 3.1 to 3.9) of section 3 of the questionnaire. Factor analysis identified item Q3.7 as clearly measuring something very different from the other items. It is not clear whether the formulation (the reference to a librarian) led students to view it differently from the other questions which are all concerned with classroom or lecturing tasks. However, in order to simplify matters, this item was dropped in subsequent analyses.

The optimal solution resulted in a three-factor structure with items 3.1 to 3.4 loading highly on the first factor, 3.5 and 3.6 on the second factor, and 3.8 and 3.9 on the third factor. The three-factor solution explains 59 per cent of the variance compared to the two-factor solution which explains 45 per cent of the variance.

On the basis of the factor-analytic results which indicated a high loading and correlation between the first four questions, it was decided to proceed with the construction of one index only. This is because it is clear from the factor analysis, that the first four questions do in fact measure something like "confidence" and a disposition to act in class.

The "confidence index" was constructed by summing the mean values for each respondent. This could vary between 1 and 5. These were re-coded as follows:

- Those who scored 2 and less were recoded as 1 (Highly confident and active),
- those who scored between 2 and 3 as 2 (Moderately confident),
- those who scored between 3 and 4 as 3 (Not very confident),
- those who scored more than 4 as 4 (Not confident at all).

The "face" validity of the index was tested by cross-tabulating the scores of students on the new index with other variables that could give an indication of whether it tells us something useful. Two cross-tabulations with race and performance were run. The same procedure as explained above was used for all the indexes that were constructed. The results of the index of confidence are produced below.

Index of confidence across institutions in the region [1]

Graph 5.1 presents results of the index of confidence across the various.institutions, thus providing a comparative look at which institutions appear to have more confident students in class. This is the only index which is based on a four-point scale and the results are in some instances reported by collapsing the last two points, viz. "not very confident" with "not confident at all and inactive". This is done to give an indication of how large a number of students feel relatively or completely unconfident in class.

CHART 5.1: Frequency count of the index of reading and writing ability

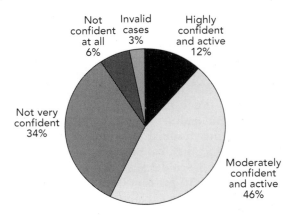

The graph below indicates a greater proportion of students at UWC (13%), CT(16%) and PT (19%) recorded higher levels of confidence than students at UCT (10%) and US (9%). The most important result is the fact that at least half of the proportion of students report not being confident. This is more marked at CT and US than at the other three institutions.

GRAPH 5.1: Institutional results of the index of confidence across the region

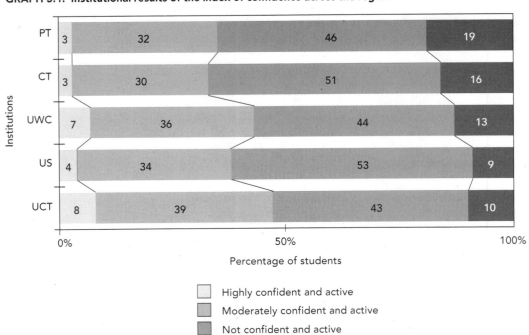

Index of academic confidence of total sample by variables

The following table (Table 5.1) suggests that confidence generally increases marginally from junior undergraduate (12%) to post-graduate level (14%). A smaller portion of postgraduate students report feeling less confident (38%)[2] than junior undergraduates (41%). The table thus reveals that confidence is in most cases related to year level, with senior students (4th year) feeling more able to engage with learning than junior undergraduates. This is unsurprising as the first-year experience is daunting and many such students are simply adjusting to higher-education life. This suggests the need for greater input and attention to the needs of first-year students.

With regard to disciplinary domains, students in the applied sciences report greater confidence (17%) than those in the humanities (13%) and social sciences (13%), and most especially students in the natural sciences (8%). An average of 42 per cent of students across all the domains report poor confidence, except for engineering and design (32%). This suggests that students across the disciplines with the possible exception of those in the applied sciences, require injections of confidence to predispose them to information-literacy competencies.

In relation to academic performance, better achievers, i.e. those scoring 70 per cent and more (19%), report high levels of confidence and have a lesser problem with low levels of confidence (26 and 4%) in comparison to those achieving less than 50%. It appears that poor academic performers are less confident and that there is a positive relationship between confidence and academic performance. For example, of those scoring less than 50 per cent, only 51 per cent of the sample report high or moderate confidence as opposed to 69 per cent of those achieving 70 per cent and more. Bearing in mind the earlier argument that confidence predisposes learners towards greater levels of information literacy, it appears that under-achievers require greater inputs in terms of developing their confidence.

As far as racial differences are concerned, a greater proportion of African students (15%) are highly confident followed by Indian (13%), white (12%) and coloured (11%) students. However, when read together with responses to moderate levels of confidence, white students (61%) take the lead, followed by African (59%), Indian (57%) and coloured students (56%). Reports of a complete lack of confidence follow similar patterns with Indian students reporting the least confidence (10%), followed by coloured and African students (both 6%) and white students (5%). When read together with students who are not very confident, a similar pattern emerges to that of year groups so that 40 per cent white, 41 per cent African, 43 per cent Indian and 44 per cent coloured students in the system report minimal confidence.

"... students in the applied sciences report greater confidence than those in the humanities and social sciences, and most especially students in the natural sciences."

A gender perspective on academic confidence shows that fewer female (10%) than male students (15%) record high confidence, and similarly 44 per cent female as opposed to 50 per cent male report moderate confidence. By contrast, 46 per cent females as opposed to 35 per cent males claim to be "not very confident" or "not confident at all and inactive". The gender differences suggest that women could be a special target group for academic-confidence development.

In terms of age, there is a striking difference in levels of confidence with students aged 30 years or older (30%) reporting high confidence as opposed to only ten per cent of those under 22 years and 16 per cent of those ranging from 22 to 29 years of age. The pattern holds for low levels of confidence with only 30 per cent of those 30 years or older claiming low levels of confidence as opposed to 42 per cent of under 22-year-olds and 40 per cent of those 22 to 29 years old.

Index of confidence by institutions and key variables

The following institutional tables (5.2–5.6) correspond with the patterns reflected in the total sample. However, the results indicate a difference between UCT and UWC on the one hand, and US, CT and PT on the other with respect to both year level and gender. Students at the former record greater levels of lack of confidence across all year groups, while the latter report higher levels of confidence. Thus, on average, US reports 37 per cent, PT 35 per cent and CT 31 per cent of students "not very confident" or "not at all confident". UCT on the other hand reports an average of 46 per cent and UWC 43 per cent for the same categories. In terms of gender, 53 per cent of female students at UCT and 46 per cent at UWC report poor academic confidence as opposed to 42 per cent and 39 per cent males respectively. By contrast, 42 per cent of women at US and PT, and 39 per cent at CT report in the same categories.

"The gender differences suggest that women could be a special target group for academic-confidence development."

With regard to disciplinary domain, UWC and UCT students in the natural sciences (only 7% highly confident in each case, and 8 and 9% not at all confident respectively) report lower levels of academic confidence than those in the total sample.

A further deviation in the institutional tables from the total sample is found in UCT's academic confidence index by race. While in the total sample African students reported highest levels of confidence for the first category of the scale ("highly confident and active"), at UCT the pattern changes with African (8%) and coloured (5%) students reporting lesser confidence than white students (13%). The pattern detected at UCT is also found at CT, although less prominently with an average of 13 per cent black as opposed to 18 per cent white reporting greatest confidence. At UCT, African and coloured students also report lack of confidence, 54 per cent and 52 per cent respectively. This underscores the need

TABLE 5.1: Index of confidence in class – Total sample

	Highly confident and active in class	Moderately confident and active in class	Not very confident	Not confident and inactive	Total count
	Row %	Row %	Row %	Row %	
Year group					
Junior undergraduate	12	47	35	6	3 179
Senior undergraduate	13	45	36	6	1 318
Postgraduate	14	48	33	5	692
Disciplinary area					
Humanities	13	43	38	6	910
Social sciences	13	44	36	6	1 225
Economic and management sciences	11	47	36	6	1 468
Natural sciences	8	47	38	6	550
Engineering and design	17	50	29	3	582
Medical and health sciences	11	52	31	6	667
Academic performance					
<50%	12	39	39	10	371
50–59%	9	46	40	6	1 587
60–69%	11	47	36	6	2 104
70%+	19	50	26	4	1 130
Race					
African	15	44	35	6	1 455
White	12	49	35	5	2 334
Coloured	11	45	38	6	1 225
Indian	13	44	33	10	230
Gender					
Female	10	44	40	6	2 888
Male	15	50	30	5	2 554
Language					
Afrikaans	9	52	34	5	1 603
English	12	45	37	5	2 244
African languages	15	45	33	6	1 419
Other languages	18	36	38	9	135
Age in years					
Under 22	10	48	36	6	3 588
22–29	16	45	35	5	1 627
30 or older	30	41	23	6	230

to focus on these constituencies at these campuses in developing academic confidence across the region.

In terms of academic performance it is important to note that a greater proportion of UCT students across all levels of achievement report less confidence than in the total sample. Particularly significant are their below 50 per cent achievers, 69 per cent of whom report lacking in confidence.

TABLE 5.2: Index of confidence in class – UCT

	Highly confident and active in class	Moderately confident and active in class	Not very confident	Not confident and inactive	Total count
	Row %	Row %	Row %	Row %	
Year group					
Junior undergraduate	10	41	40	9	937
Senior undergraduate	10	45	40	5	352
Postgraduate	11	46	37	6	405
Disciplinary area					
Humanities	13	42	39	7	409
Social sciences	11	40	41	8	327
Economic and management sciences	11	41	42	6	403
Natural sciences	7	39	45	9	214
Engineering and design	—	—	—	—	—
Medical and health sciences	7	53	32	8	339
Academic performance					
<50%	8	23	51	18	84
50–59%	7	37	45	11	329
60–69%	8	45	41	6	743
70%+	17	49	30	4	463
Race					
African	8	39	44	10	405
White	13	44	38	5	892
Coloured	5	42	43	9	217
Indian	12	46	30	11	115
Gender					
Female	8	39	44	9	916
Male	13	47	34	6	773
Language					
Afrikaans	14	43	36	7	72
English	10	44	39	6	1 135
African languages	8	40	42	10	378
Other languages	14	35	38	12	97
Age in years					
Under 22	9	43	39	8	1 149
22–29	11	43	40	6	495
30 or older	23	34	38	4	47

The results for the index of confidence indicate noteworthy differences in the levels of confidence reported by the students with as many as 33 per cent of the proportion of students in the sample reporting low levels of confidence. In particular poor academic performers and female students express a greater lack of academic confidence than the rest of the student body. These are clearly target groups among whom information literacy has to be promoted

TABLE 5.3: Index of confidence in class – US

	Highly confident and active in class	Moderately confident and active in class	Not very confident	Not confident and inactive	Total count
	Row %	Row %	Row %	Row %	
Year group					
Junior undergraduate	8	53	34	5	984
Senior undergraduate	9	49	35	7	179
Postgraduate	12	57	29	2	184
Disciplinary area					
Humanities	10	47	38	6	200
Social sciences	9	49	36	6	329
Economic and management sciences	8	54	34	5	450
Natural sciences	10	61	28	2	184
Engineering and design	—	—	—	—	—
Medical and health sciences	9	63	26	2	110
Academic performance					
<50%	10	44	38	8	89
50–59%	5	50	41	4	357
60–69%	8	55	32	5	500
70%+	13	58	26	3	290
Race					
African	14	48	33	5	21
White	8	54	33	5	1 061
Coloured	8	49	39	4	160
Indian	38	50	—	13	8
Gender					
Female	8	50	37	5	779
Male	10	58	29	4	492
Language					
Afrikaans	8	57	30	4	838
English	9	45	41	6	382
African languages	21	58	16	5	19
Other languages	18	41	41	—	17
Age in years					
Under 22	8	53	35	5	1 052
22–29	11	53	33	4	190
30 or older	38	52	7	3	29

within an overall programme of information-literacy education that serves to boost confidence by equipping students with the tools and skills to perform effectively in this environment.

Index of reading and writing ability

In designing the questionnaire, it was assumed that the set of items Q4.1 to 4.6 all measure the ability or competence of students with

TABLE 5.4: Index of confidence in class – UWC

	Highly confident and active in class	Moderately confident and active in class	Not very confident	Not confident and inactive	Total count
	Row %	Row %	Row %	Row %	
Year group					
Junior undergraduate	14	45	34	7	546
Senior undergraduate	12	42	38	8	460
Postgraduate	14	43	35	8	210
Disciplinary area					
Humanities	15	43	37	5	301
Social sciences	15	45	33	8	341
Economic and management sciences	12	45	35	8	372
Natural sciences	7	43	42	8	152
Engineering and design	—	—	—	—	—
Medical and health sciences	22	33	29	16	49
Academic performance					
<50%	18	35	38	9	94
50–59%	9	47	38	6	520
60–69%	14	42	36	8	407
70%+	23	43	24	11	131
Race					
African	15	46	32	7	616
White	13	88	—	—	8
Coloured	12	39	41	9	439
Indian	10	41	38	10	99
Gender					
Female	10	43	39	7	671
Male	17	44	31	8	539
Language					
Afrikaans	8	37	42	13	238
English	14	42	38	6	340
African languages	16	47	31	6	611
Other languages	33	33	33	—	6
Age in years					
Under 22	10	44	37	9	588
22–29	15	45	35	5	536
30 or older	27	39	25	8	84

regard to reading and writing. The factor analysis showed that only one question did not fit the overall pattern. The particular item on students' ability to prepare references (item Q4.6) loaded on a different dimension to the five other items and was therefore dropped from subsequent analyses. Once this was done, a single-factor solution was obtained which explained 43 per cent of the variance in the responses. A similar procedure as before was followed in construct-

TABLE 5.5: Index of confidence in class – CT

	Highly confident and active in class	Moderately confident and active in class	Not very confident	Not confident and inactive	Total count
	Row %	Row %	Row %	Row %	
Year group					
Junior undergraduate	13	51	32	3	404
Senior undergraduate	16	50	30	4	115
Postgraduate	27	48	23	2	94
Disciplinary area					
Humanities	—	—	—	—	—
Social sciences	21	48	29	2	58
Economic and management sciences	16	53	28	3	155
Natural sciences	—	—	—	—	—
Engineering and design	13	50	32	4	312
Medical and health sciences	9	59	32	—	34
Academic performance					
<50%	11	49	36	4	45
50–59%	7	50	40	3	166
60–69%	15	52	27	5	233
70%+	25	50	23	2	152
Race					
African	16	51	28	5	107
White	18	48	31	3	365
Coloured	9	58	30	3	121
Indian	29	43	29	—	7
Gender					
Female	18	44	35	4	228
Male	14	55	27	3	383
Language					
Afrikaans	12	52	32	4	234
English	18	51	29	3	263
African languages	17	50	28	5	102
Other languages	18	36	45	—	11
Age in years					
Under 22	9	55	32	4	423
22–29	29	40	28	3	145
30 or older	33	42	22	2	45

ing a composite index of reading and writing ability. The mean scores of individual respondents were summed. These could range between 1 and 3. Three new categories were formed and the distribution on these is given in Chart 5.2 below.

Cross-tabulations were run with race and performance to check the face validity of this index.

TABLE 5.6: Index of confidence in class – PT

	Highly confident and active in class	Moderately confident and active in class	Not very confident	Not confident and inactive	Total count
	Row %	Row %	Row %	Row %	
Year group					
Junior undergraduate	18	48	32	3	384
Senior undergraduate	21	44	33	3	212
Postgraduate	22	43	33	1	69
Disciplinary area					
Humanities	—	—	—	—	—
Social sciences	18	41	38	4	170
Economic and management sciences	16	41	40	3	88
Natural sciences	—	—	—	—	—
Engineering and design	22	50	26	2	270
Medical and health sciences	17	47	33	3	135
Academic performance					
<50%	12	53	29	7	59
50–59%	17	45	35	3	215
60–69%	16	45	37	3	221
70%+	33	46	20	1	94
Race					
African	23	44	31	—	59
White	50	25	25	3	215
Coloured	15	48	34	3	221
Indian	100	—	—	—	94
Gender					
Female	15	43	39	3	294
Male	23	49	26	3	367
Language					
Afrikaans	10	49	39	—	221
English	25	49	23	3	124
African languages	23	43	31	2	309
Other languages	75	25	—	3	4
Age in years					
Under 22	16	47	34	3	376
22–29	22	44	31	3	261
30 or older	32	48	12	8	25

Index of reading and writing ability across institutions in the region

Graph 5.2 provides an overview of the index of reading and writing ability by institution. The graph suggests substantive differences between HDIs and HAIs, in that fewer students at UWC and PT record never or rarely having difficulties with reading and writing (UWC 24 % and PT 29% respectively of their proportion

CHART 5.2: Frequency count of the index of reading and writing ability across the region

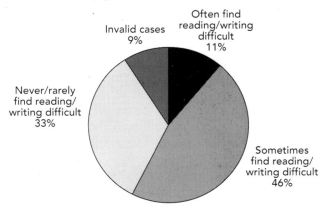

of students in the sample) compared to a greater proportion of students at the three HAIs (UCT 39%, US 46% and CT 43% of their proportion of students sampled). If one considers race, the results indicate that across all institutions black students report greater difficulty with reading and writing. The interesting feature is that in the category "often" UCT's results are similar to the HDIs. This is possibly due to the high proportion of black students at UCT.

GRAPH 5.2: Institutional results of the index of reading and writing ability in the region

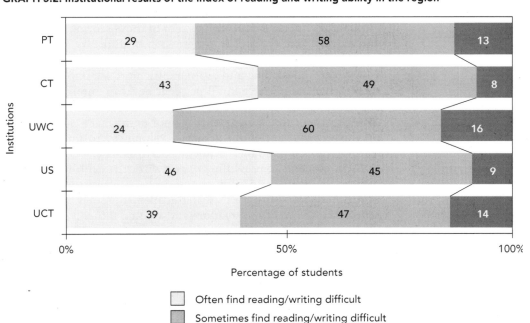

Index of reading and writing ability of the total sample

The index of reading and writing in Table 5.7 indicates that more senior undergraduates (14%) than junior undergraduates (12%) and postgraduates (11%) often find reading and writing difficult. Accordingly, they show the lowest percentage of those never finding reading and writing difficult: 33 per cent as opposed to 36 per cent of junior undergraduates and 43 per cent of postgraduates. One might argue that with every year of study, students become more aware of their inadequacies with regard to academic literacy, before they turn more able and confident. Should this be the case, students would require more information-literacy education in their first years of study.

"... with every year of study, students become more aware of their inadequacies with regard to academic literacy, before they turn more able and confident."

The disciplinary domains variable shows that it is mostly students in the social sciences (16%) who often find reading and writing difficult, followed by students in the humanities (13%), and in the applied and medical sciences (both 11%), and finally students in the natural sciences (10%). Students in the social sciences also report the fewest cases of never finding reading and writing difficult (29%) as opposed to those in the humanities and natural sciences (both 36%), the applied sciences (38%) and economic and management sciences (39%), as well as the medical and health sciences (46%). While these differences between disciplinary domains, it is important to note that the differences are not large.

The academic-literacy index shows a strong relationship with academic performance. Poor academic achievers experience more difficulty with reading and writing than those who score well. Twenty per cent of those scoring less than 50 per cent often have difficulty as opposed to seven per cent of those scoring 70 per cent and more. There is a steady progression of difficulty experienced by students between these levels. The same pattern holds for those who never find reading and writing difficult. Fifty-two per cent of those achieving more than 70 per cent never or rarely have difficulty as opposed to 23 per cent who score less than 50 per cent. This consistent trend suggests that poor performers require greatest inputs of information-literacy development to improve their learning capacity and their academic performance.

Black students express the greatest difficulty with reading and writing (on average 15%) in comparison to white students (8%). White students also report greater academic literacy with 50 per cent never or rarely find reading and writing difficult as opposed to an average of 27 per cent of black students. These patterns illustrate greater levels of need for academic-literacy development among black students.

More female students report lower levels of academic literacy than male students: 14 per cent females often have difficulties as opposed to 11 per cent males, and only 34 per cent females as opposed to 40 per cent males never have difficulties. This pattern is consistent with other indexes where female students usually report greater levels of need in terms of information-literacy nterventions and development.

The results indicate that African-language students have greatest difficulty with reading and writing; 16 per cent in comparison to 10 per cent English-speakers and 11 per cent Afrikaans-speakers. This pattern is consistent in terms of those who never or rarely find reading and writing difficult: only 24 per cent of African-language speakers as opposed to 38 per cent of Afrikaans- and 40 per cent of English-speakers never have difficulties. This variable supports previous conclusions for this index, viz. that black students generally require greater information-literacy development, and that of these, African-language speakers are a significant group.

The results for age indicates that older students generally have greater difficulties with reading and writing than those under 22 years. Seventeen per cent of those 30 years and older as opposed to 11 per cent of those under 22 express most difficulty, with the pattern holding for minimal difficulty: only 30 per cent of older students never have difficulty as opposed to 38 per cent of younger students. This feature might be due to the fact that younger students might not have had a gap in their formal education while older students may often be returning students who have not practised their academic-literacy skills for a while.

Index of reading and writing ability by institutions and key variables

Tables 5.8 to 5.12 provide a closer institutional profile of the index of reading and writing ability.

The tables indicate that UCT's senior undergraduates record higher reading and writing ability in that 42 per cent of them, as opposed to only 33 per cent in the total sample, never or rarely have difficulty with reading and writing. US students across all year groups report less difficulty with academic literacy than reported in the total sample. For example, as little as five per cent of the postgraduate sample, as opposed to 11 per cent of the total postgraduate sample, often find difficulty, while 58 per cent as opposed to 43 per cent at this level report not having difficulty. Similarly, only nine per cent of both their junior and senior undergraduates, as opposed to 12 and 14 per cent respectively, often find reading and writing difficult, while 44 and 42 per cent in these categories, as opposed to 36 and 33 per cent, never report difficulty. While CT undergraduate students report similarly to   US students – except for their senior undergraduates, 12 per cent of whom report often finding reading and writing difficult – UWC and PT report lower levels of academic literacy than the total sample. At both these institutions, fewer students report never or rarely having difficulties with reading and writing. UWC's undergraduate results are particularly weak, with only 23 per cent junior and 22 per cent senior undergraduates reporting never or rarely finding reading and writing difficult. As noted in the total sample, there appears to be a marked

TABLE 5.7: Index of reading and writing ability – Total sample

	Often find reading and writing difficult	Sometimes find reading and writing difficult	Never/rarely find reading and writing difficult	Total count
	Row %	Row %	Row %	Row %
Year group				
Junior undergraduate	14	54	33	1 344
Senior undergraduate	11	46	43	988
Postgraduate	13	51	36	936
Disciplinary area				
Humanities	13	51	36	936
Social sciences	16	55	29	1 262
Economic and management sciences	11	51	38	1 497
Natural sciences	10	54	36	570
Engineering and design	11	50	39	594
Medical and health sciences	11	43	46	686
Academic performance				
<50%	20	57	23	386
50–59%	16	56	28	1 633
60–69%	11	51	38	2 142
70%+	7	41	52	1 159
Race				
African	16	60	24	1 527
White	8	42	50	2 368
Coloured	15	57	28	1 256
Indian	13	57	30	232
Gender				
Female	14	52	34	2 972
Male	11	50	40	2 614
Language				
Afrikaans	11	51	38	1 624
English	10	46	44	2 279
African languages	16	60	24	1 491
Other languages	12	48	40	139
Age in years				
Under 22	11	51	38	3 667
22–29	14	52	34	1 678
30 or older	17	53	30	244

divide between the HDIs and the HAIs with significantly more students at the former reporting low levels of academic literacy.

The results for academic performance indicate a similar difference between HDIs and HAIs as found in relation to year group. Fewer students at UWC and PT report never or rarely having difficulty with reading and writing than those at UCT, US and CT, although only 16 per cent of UCT students who score under 50 per cent report never having difficulty. Also, more of these

UCT students and those achieving between 50 and 59 per cent report often finding difficulty.

The gender results in relation to this index suggest that fewer students, both male and female, from UWC and PT rarely find reading and writing difficult and that at UWC the gap between male and female reporting (30:20%) is wider than that in the total sample.

As far as language is concerned, more Afrikaans-speakers (22%) than in the total sample (11%) often find reading and writing difficult, and far fewer of these students (17%) than that in the total sample (38%) never have difficulty. UCT also shows that more Afrikaans- (16%) and African-language speakers (23%) than those in the total sample (11 and 16% respectively) have greater difficulty with reading and writing.

US and CT appear to report greater levels of academic literacy across age groups in that fewer students have difficulty (on average 9 and 10% respectively), and more students rarely have difficulty (on average 42 and 37% respectively) with reading and writing than those reported in the total sample. By contrast, students at UWC and PT (27 and 30% respectively) both report lower percentages of students across the ages never having difficulty with reading and writing. UCT also reports the most mature students (27% as opposed to 17% in the total sample) as often finding reading and writing difficult, and fewest in this category never having difficulty (only 22% as opposed to 30% in the total sample).

"The biggest concern ... is the fact that the results for the sample across all variables indicate that only a third of all students experience no reading and writing difficulties."

The picture that emerges is that black students report greater reading and writing difficulties than their white counterparts. With the exception of CT, a greater proportion of female students report difficulties than males.

The biggest concern, however, is the fact that the results for the sample across all variables indicate that only a third of all students experience no reading and writing difficulties. This is more evident at the two HDIs than the three HAIs. The findings suggest that in terms of academic literacy, black students and female students require greatest information-literacy development.

Index of computer competence

The index of computer competence is based on items Q4.7 to 4.14 of the questionnaire. The index thus excludes questions on access to computers and facilities such as the Internet (item 4.15). The latter are specifically about access to the Internet and other computing facilities rather than usage or competence. These questions are not lost in the analysis and are discussed in relation to individual institutional profiles (see Chapter 5) and predictor variable analysis (see Chapter 6).

A factor analysis of the eight items reveals an interesting two-factor solution which explains nearly 62 per cent of the variance

TABLE 5.8: Index of reading and writing ability – UCT

	Often find reading and writing difficult	Sometimes find reading and writing difficult	Never/rarely find reading and writing difficult	Total count
	Row %	Row %	Row %	
Year group				
Junior undergraduate	16	49	35	968
Senior undergraduate	12	46	42	356
Postgraduate	12	43	45	417
Disciplinary area				
Humanities	13	44	43	423
Social sciences	20	50	30	331
Economic and management sciences	13	49	38	413
Natural sciences	13	51	36	222
Engineering and design	—	—	—	—
Medical and health sciences	12	42	46	350
Academic performance				
<50%	28	56	16	89
50–59%	23	51	26	340
60–69%	13	48	39	758
70%+	7	38	54	473
Race				
African	22	56	22	424
White	8	41	51	908
Coloured	19	55	26	226
Indian	20	49	31	116
Gender				
Female	15	49	36	935
Male	13	44	43	800
Language				
Afrikaans	16	49	34	73
English	11	44	45	1 154
African languages	23	56	21	395
Other languages	15	48	37	100
Age in years				
Under 22	13	47	39	1 178
22–29	15	45	40	511
30 or older	27	51	22	49

in the data. The factor structure is interesting because it indicates that the first three items (computer-operating system, word-processing and spreadsheet) cluster together, and that the remaining items constitute a second factor. However, it should be added that item Q4.14 on CD-ROM loads highly on both factors. It is likely that this result indicates that "complexity" or "degree of difficulty" is in fact the basis for the division into two factors. The first factor consists of the three most commonly used computer

TABLE 5.9 Index of reading and writing ability – US

	Often find reading and writing difficult	Sometimes find reading and writing difficult	Never/rarely find reading and writing difficult	Total count
	Row %	Row %	Row %	
Year group				
Junior undergraduate	9	47	44	922
Senior undergraduate	9	49	42	182
Postgraduate	5	36	58	187
Disciplinary area				
Humanities	11	48	42	204
Social sciences	11	50	39	335
Economic and management sciences	8	43	48	457
Natural sciences	6	49	45	185
Engineering and design	—	—	—	—
Medical and health sciences	2	29	69	112
Academic performance				
<50%	19	49	32	90
50–59%	10	49	41	365
60–69%	8	48	44	505
70%+	6	34	60	295
Race				
African	14	59	27	22
White	8	43	49	1 077
Coloured	10	59	31	162
Indian	25	38	38	8
Gender				
Female	10	45	45	791
Male	6	46	47	499
Language				
Afrikaans	7	46	47	845
English	10	44	46	389
African languages	15	70	15	20
Other languages	6	33	61	18
Age in years				
Under 22	9	46	45	1 068
22–29	8	38	54	193
30 or older	10	62	28	29

applications, whereas the second factor consists of four more uncommon and unfamiliar applications – databases, graphics programmes, statistical packages and CAD packages, where CD-ROM could fit in as well.

This suggests that these results could indicate an underlying single dimension. In fact, an enforced one-factor solution still explains 45 per cent of the variance in the data. On this basis a "computer-competence index" was constructed. The index was

TABLE 5.10: Index of reading and writing ability – UWC

	Often find reading and writing difficult	Sometimes find reading and writing difficult	Never/rarely find reading and writing difficult	Total count
	Row %	Row %	Row %	
Year group				
Junior undergraduate	14	62	23	580
Senior undergraduate	17	60	22	470
Postgraduate	16	52	32	212
Disciplinary area				
Humanities	15	62	23	309
Social sciences	19	57	24	355
Economic and management sciences	16	61	23	383
Natural sciences	11	63	26	163
Engineering and design	—	—	—	—
Medical and health sciences	10	53	37	51
Academic performance				
<50%	19	70	11	99
50–59%	17	63	21	536
60–69%	17	55	29	416
70%+	8	56	36	140
Race				
African	15	62	23	646
White	38	38	25	8
Coloured	18	57	25	451
Indian	6	67	27	100
Gender				
Female	19	61	20	705
Male	12	58	30	550
Language				
Afrikaans	22	61	17	245
English	13	56	31	344
African languages	15	62	23	642
Other languages	—	67	33	6
Age in years				
Under 22	14	63	24	608
22–29	18	59	24	554
30 or older	16	48	35	91

based on the first three response categories of each item only. It is clear from the items that the four response options do not constitute a linear scale. The difference between the last two options "Unable to use but would like to" and "Unable to use but do not need/want to" is important. In order, therefore, not to confound these differences into one index, it was decided to only include those cases which utilised the first three response categories. Again, a sum of the mean scores was computed for each response.

TABLE 5.11: Index of reading and writing ability -- CT

	Often find reading and writing difficult	Sometimes find reading and writing difficult	Never/rarely find reading and writing difficult	Total count
	Row %	Row %	Row %	
Year group				
Junior undergraduate	6	50	44	411
Senior undergraduate	12	46	43	120
Postgraduate	12	48	39	97
Disciplinary area				
Humanities	—	—	—	—
Social sciences	10	65	26	62
Economic and management sciences	3	51	46	155
Natural sciences	—	—	—	—
Engineering and design	9	46	45	318
Medical and health sciences	3	47	50	36
Academic performance				
<50%	8	58	33	48
50–59%	11	55	34	167
60–69%	7	51	42	238
70%+	7	38	54	156
Race				
African	11	60	29	117
White	8	43	49	367
Coloured	7	58	35	123
Indian	—	57	43	7
Gender				
Female	8	53	39	234
Male	8	47	45	392
Language				
Afrikaans	10	50	40	236
English	5	45	50	266
African languages	11	59	30	112
Other languages	9	55	36	11
Age in years				
Under 22	7	47	46	428
22–29	9	52	38	149
30 or older	14	59	27	51

These could vary between 1 and 3 and were re-coded as follows:

- Values ranging between 1 and 1.7 were re-coded as "1"
- Values ranging between 1.7 and 2.4 were re-coded as "2"
- Values ranging between 2.4 and 3 were re-coded as "3"

The results of the re-coding are presented in Chart 5.3.

TABLE 5.12: Index of reading and writing ability – PT

	Often find reading and writing difficult	Sometimes find reading and writing difficult	Never/rarely find reading and writing difficult	Total count
	Row %	Row %	Row %	
Year group				
Junior undergraduate	14	55	31	393
Senior undergraduate	13	61	25	216
Postgraduate	9	68	23	75
Disciplinary area				
Humanities	—	—	—	—
Social sciences	12	65	23	179
Economic and management sciences	13	58	28	89
Natural sciences	—	—	—	—
Engineering and design	13	55	31	276
Medical and health sciences	16	53	31	137
Academic performance				
<50%	14	61	25	318
50–59%	—	50	50	8
60–69%	14	58	29	294
70%+	—	100	—	1
Race				
African	11	60	29	117
White	8	43	49	367
Coloured	7	58	35	123
Indian	—	57	43	7
Gender				
Female	14	60	25	307
Male	13	57	31	373
Language				
Afrikaans	15	62	24	225
English	12	46	42	126
African languages	14	60	27	322
Other languages	—	75	25	4
Age in years				
Under 22	13	58	29	385
22–29	14	58	28	271
30 or older	13	54	33	24

Index of computer competence across the region by institution

Graph 5.3 provides the results for the index of computer competence by institution. The results for the index indicate a clear difference between the HDIs and HAIs. A smaller proportion of students at UWC and PT are computer literate (8% of the proportion of students in each case) than those at UCT (16%), CT (18%)

CHART 5.3: Frequency count of the index of computer competence in the region

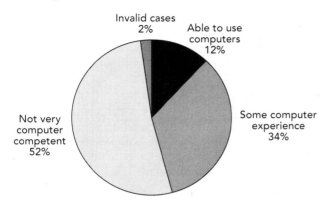

and US (11%). It is interesting to note that UWC is the weakest institution in this regard with as many as two-thirds (67%) of the proportion of students reporting minimal computer competence. The regional situation suggests that in the area of computer competence, the HDIs require greater levels of information-literacy advancement than other institutions.

GRAPH 5.3: Institutional results of the index of computer competence

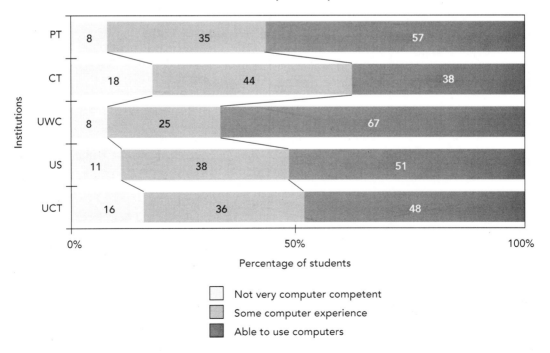

Index of computer competence of the total sample

Table 5.13 reflects the index of computer competence in the total sample surveyed by each of the variables listed.

There are no important and obvious differences in computer competence across year groups, nor across age groups, although older students seem more able to use computers (15%) than those under 22 (12%).

Computer competence by disciplinary domain shows that students in the applied sciences are most computer-competent: 17 per cent are able to use computers, while 39 per cent report not being very computer-competent. By comparison, ten per cent in the humanities are able to use computers, while as many as 66 per cent are not very computer-competent. This difference in levels in computer competence across the domains clearly has to do with the nature of the discipline. Students in engineering and design are more likely to be required to use computer applications than their counterparts in the humanities and social sciences.

It is interesting to note that students achieving 70 per cent and more report greater computer competence (16% able and 45% limited) as opposed to those scoring less than 50 per cent (13% able and 58% limited competence). This seems to indicate that in terms of this aspect of information literacy, the higher achievers are more information-literate than those scoring less than 70 per cent.

"This difference in levels in computer competence across the domains clearly has to do with the nature of the discipline."

Analysis by race indicates that black students are less computer-competent than white students with only eight per cent coloured, ten per cent African and 11 per cent Indian students reporting ability as opposed to 16 per cent of white students. Similarly, black students record the higher percentages of need in this area (63% African, 60% coloured and 58% Indian) in contrast to 44 per cent white students. Again, it appears that the index of confidence, which reported greater confidence among black students than white students, does not translate into computer competence.

The gender differences in terms of the computer competence index is important in that only seven per cent female students report computer competence in comparison to 19 per cent male, and 62 per cent of women report not being very computer-competent as opposed to 43 per cent males.

As in other instances, language appears to be related to race in that African-language speakers report higher incidence of computer incompetence (63%) with Afrikaans-speakers at 53 per cent and English-speakers at 48 per cent.

Index of computer competence by institutions and key variables

Tables 5.14 to 5.18 display the institutional profiles of the index of computer competence by key variables.

In terms of year group, computer ability declines across the three year levels at the universities whereas at the technikons, it

TABLE 5.13: Index of computer competence – Total sample

	Ability to use computers	Some experience in computers	Not very computer-competent	Total count
	Row %	Row %	Row %	
Year group				
Junior undergraduate	13	33	54	3 167
Senior undergraduate	12	36	52	1 326
Postgraduate	14	34	52	971
Disciplinary area				
Humanities	10	24	66	898
Social sciences	9	29	62	1 226
Economic and management sciences	15	44	42	1 471
Natural sciences	13	33	53	556
Engineering and design	17	44	39	582
Medical and health sciences	12	29	59	671
Academic performance				
<50%	13	28	58	372
50–59%	11	33	57	1 576
60–69%	13	34	53	2 099
70%+	16	39	45	1 148
Race				
African	10	27	63	1 457
White	16	40	44	2 335
Coloured	8	32	60	1 228
Indian	11	31	58	227
Gender				
Female	7	30	62	2 897
Male	19	38	43	2 547
Language				
Afrikaans	10	36	53	1 599
English	15	37	48	2 242
African languages	11	27	63	1 416
Other languages	18	36	47	135
Age in years				
Under 22	12	35	53	3 579
22–29	14	32	54	1 635
30 or older	15	32	52	234

increases. Thus, postgraduate (4th year) students at universities report being less able to use computers than first-year students. A possible explanation is the fact that students who have recently entered universities have been more exposed to computers than those who entered at least three years ago. Technikon students are probably more able to use computers due to the heavy emphasis placed on technology in the respective disciplines at these institutions.

TABLE 5.14: Index of computer competence – UCT

	Ability to use computers	Some experience in computers	Not very computer-competent	Total count
	Row %	Row %	Row %	
Year group				
Junior undergraduate	17	35	48	950
Senior undergraduate	17	42	42	350
Postgraduate	15	35	51	413
Disciplinary area				
Humanities	13	30	57	413
Social sciences	11	34	55	325
Economic and management sciences	25	47	28	409
Natural sciences	18	40	43	221
Engineering and design	—	—	—	—
Medical and health sciences	—	—	—	—
Academic performance				
<50%	17	22	61	89
50–59%	15	38	47	327
60–69%	15	35	50	747
70%+	19	40	41	472
Race				
African	13	31	56	410
White	19	42	40	902
Coloured	13	26	62	221
Indian	14	35	51	113
Gender				
Female	9	35	56	921
Male	25	38	37	785
Language				
Afrikaans	14	32	54	72
English	18	38	44	1 143
African languages	13	30	57	381
Other languages	18	35	47	97
Age in years				
Under 22	16	37	47	1 160
22–29	16	35	49	502
30 or older	17	33	50	48

In terms of race, it is evident from the tables that black (coloured and African) students are not as computer-competent as white students. US is the exception, but here the number of African students is very low (N = 21). It is interesting to note that the black UCT students boost the total sample reports for computer competence with more black students at this institution reporting an ability to use computers than in the total sample. Interestingly, CT shows that the racial divide between black and

TABLE 5.15: Index of computer competence – US

	Ability to use computers	Some experience in computers	Not very computer-competent	Total count
	Row %	Row %	Row %	
Year group				
Junior undergraduate	12	33	55	900
Senior undergraduate	10	41	49	181
Postgraduate	10	39	52	186
Disciplinary area				
Humanities	11	21	68	197
Social sciences	8	29	63	328
Economic and management sciences	14	47	39	450
Natural sciences	10	35	54	184
Engineering and design	—	—	—	—
Medical and health sciences	13	31	56	110
Academic performance				
<50%	11	39	49	87
50–59%	12	37	50	358
60–69%	11	33	56	495
70%+	11	36	53	293
Race				
African	14	43	43	21
White	11	36	53	1 057
Coloured	8	29	64	159
Indian	25	38	38	8
Gender				
Female	7	31	62	774
Male	18	42	40	492
Language				
Afrikaans	11	35	54	834
English	11	34	55	378
African languages	26	37	37	19
Other languages	11	50	39	18
Age in years				
Under 22	11	34	55	1 046
22–29	15	38	47	191
30 or older	10	59	31	29

white students in relation to computer competence is striking. Very few black students (10% African and 11% coloured) in comparison to white students (24%) report an ability to use computers. Similarly, many more African (57%) and coloured (50%) students at this institution report low levels of computer competence as opposed to white students (29%). The HDIs compare poorly with the HAIs in terms of computer competence. At US, fewer white students (11%) report an ability to use computers

TABLE 5.16: Index of computer competence – UWC

	Ability to use computers	Some experience in computers	Not very computer-competent	Total count
	Row %	Row %	Row %	
Year group				
Junior undergraduate	9	23	67	539
Senior undergraduate	7	27	66	460
Postgraduate	9	24	67	203
Disciplinary area				
Humanities	7	16	77	288
Social sciences	9	23	69	340
Economic and management sciences	8	36	56	372
Natural sciences	11	21	68	151
Engineering and design	—	—	—	—
Medical and health sciences	14	16	70	50
Academic performance				
<50%	11	25	64	92
50–59%	7	25	68	509
60–69%	8	24	68	401
70%+	11	28	61	134
Race				
African	9	22	68	606
White	25	50	25	8
Coloured	7	27	66	437
Indian	8	24	67	98
Gender				
Female	6	23	71	238
Male	12	27	61	520
Language				
Afrikaans	5	26	69	238
English	9	27	63	335
African languages	9	22	68	598
Other languages	—	33	67	6
Age in years				
Under 22	7	25	68	578
22–29	9	24	67	530
30 or older	14	26	60	85

than in the total sample (16%), and more express computer incompetence (53%) than in the total sample (44%).

Computer usage is related to gender differences. Without exception, a higher proportion of males reported being able to use computers than females. For example, at UCT nine per cent of females report being able to use computers compared to 25 per cent males.

Computer ability also appears to be directly linked to disciplinary domain. For example, humanities and social sciences

TABLE 5.17: Index of computer competence – CT

	Ability to use computers	Some experience in computers	Not very computer-competent	Total count
	Row %	Row %	Row %	
Year group				
Junior undergraduate	13	43	44	398
Senior undergraduate	25	51	24	120
Postgraduate	32	38	30	96
Disciplinary area				
Humanities	—	—	—	—
Social sciences	9	33	59	58
Economic and management sciences	12	57	31	155
Natural sciences	—	—	—	—
Engineering and design	24	44	33	312
Medical and health sciences	3	15	82	33
Academic performance				
<50%	13	36	51	45
50–59%	11	34	55	63
60–69%	19	48	32	234
70%+	26	50	24	155
Race				
African	10	33	57	112
White	24	48	29	360
Coloured	11	40	50	121
Indian	—	57	43	7
Gender				
Female	8	39	54	226
Male	25	47	29	386
Language				
Afrikaans	18	49	33	234
English	21	44	35	260
African languages	8	35	57	106
Other languages	45	27	27	11
Age in years				
Under 22	15	47	39	417
22–29	27	40	33	147
30 or older	22	30	48	50

students report being less able to use computers than students in the economic and management sciences.

A regional picture shows that at least 40 per cent of the sample is not very competent in computer usage. This result is starkest at UWC and PT where, for example, 68 per cent and 61 per cent of students respectively, report not being able to use computers competently.

The findings for this index highlight racial differences, educational background and institutional location in student responses.

TABLE 5.18: Index of computer competence – PT

	Ability to use computers	Some experience in computers	Not very computer-competent	Total count
	Row %	Row %	Row %	
Year group				
Junior undergraduate	7	33	60	380
Senior undergraduate	8	35	56	215
Postgraduate	12	47	41	73
Disciplinary area				
Humanities	—	—	—	—
Social sciences	10	29	61	175
Economic and management sciences	6	20	74	85
Natural sciences	—	—	—	—
Engineering and design	9	44	47	270
Medical and health sciences	5	33	61	135
Academic performance				
<50%	14	22	64	59
50–59%	9	36	55	219
60–69%	8	37	55	222
70%+	5	44	51	94
Race				
African	9	29	62	308
White	—	63	38	8
Coloured	7	42	51	290
Indian	—	—	100	1
Gender				
Female	7	27	65	301
Male	9	41	50	364
Language				
Afrikaans	6	41	53	221
English	9	42	49	126
African languages	10	28	63	312
Other languages	—	—	100	3
Age in years				
Under 22	6	36	58	378
22–29	11	34	55	265
30 or older	9	27	64	22

It is important to note that black students, female students, poor academic performers and, in particular, students at UWC and PT require extensive computer training across a number of disciplines. Development programmes should attempt to articulate the needs of these "groupings" in promoting information-literacy activities.

Index of library usage

Nine questions were included in the survey to assess the extent to which students make use of various library facilities (items Q4.21 to 4.29). As with previous indexes, the intention was to establish the factor structure of this set of questions.

A single-factor solution, explaining 39 per cent of the variance, was generated. Sufficiently high item-factor loadings were obtained, with the exception of item Q4.27 (Used CD-ROMs in the library). If this item is deleted from the analysis, the explained variance increases to 42 per cent. Another point worth noting is that the other item which loads relatively weakly on the underlying factor is item Q4.25 (using a card catalogue). This is a potentially confounding variable since many students do not use card catalogues any more (62% of respondents indicated that they never use a card catalogue). If this item is eliminated, we find an increase in the explained variance (46%) and higher overall loadings for the other items.

Against this background, an index of library usage was constructed, on the basis of the reduced number of items. A similar procedure was followed as before.

The results of the index construction are presented in Chart 5.4 below. It reveals that most students in the sample use the library either frequently or moderately. "Frequently" means at least once a month, but most likely more often. "Moderate use" means at least once a semester but most likely more often.

CHART 5.4: Frequency count of the index of library usage

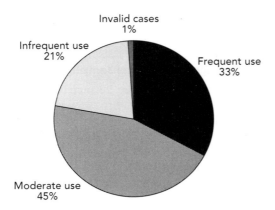

Invalid cases
1%

Infrequent use
21%

Frequent use
33%

Moderate use
45%

Index of library usage across institutions in the region

Graph 5.4 below provides a breakdown of the index of library usage by institution. The table suggests a similar pattern at UCT, UWC and PT with a greater proportion of students at these institutions reporting frequent library usage (37, 38 and 45% respectively) than those at US (19%) and CT (28%). The pattern holds for "infrequent use" with a smaller proportion of students at UCT, UWC and PT in this category (17, 19 and 11% respectively). In the latter instance, CT is not far behind the three institutions (22%), but US is different from the other institutions. At US, only 19 per cent of the sample use the library frequently while a greater proportion of students use it infrequently (35%). This regional profile, when qualified by that of the total sample, shows that black students use the library more frequently than white students.

GRAPH 5.4: Institutional results of the index of library usage across the region

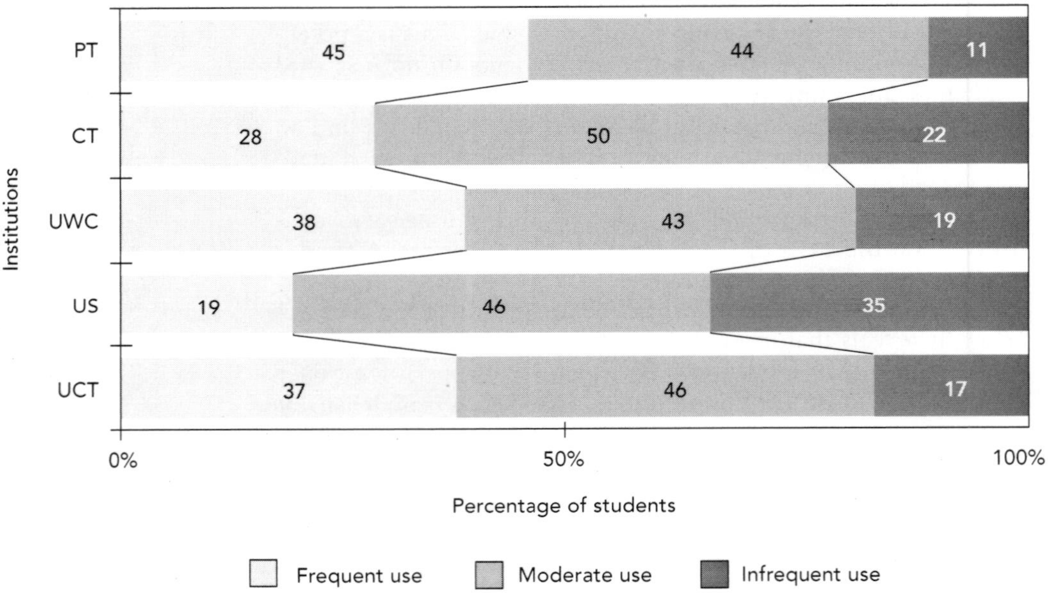

Percentage of students

☐ Frequent use   ▨ Moderate use   ■ Infrequent use

Index of library usage of the total sample

Table 5.19 indicates that library usage increases across the year level with more postgraduate students (41%) reporting frequent library use than the undergraduate group (29%). Of particular concern is the fact that 26 per cent of junior undergraduate students report using the library infrequently compared to 16 per cent of the postgraduate cohort.

It is important to note that patterns of library usage reflect a disciplinary domain difference with students in the humanities (47%) and social sciences (42%) using the library more frequently than those in the natural sciences (20%) and medical and health sciences (28%).

Perhaps the most important result is that patterns of library usage are strongly related to reported academic performance. Thus, students reporting marks of 70 per cent or higher (34%) are more frequent library users than those in the range below 50 per cent (27%).

TABLE 5.19: Index of library usage – Total sample

	Frequent use	Moderate use	Infrequent use	Total count
	Row %	Row %	Row %	
Year group				
Junior undergraduate	29	45	26	3 237
Senior undergraduate	35	50	15	1 347
Postgraduate	41	43	16	980
Disciplinary area				
Humanities	47	42	11	932
Social sciences	42	42	16	1 253
Economic and management sciences	23	47	29	1 482
Natural sciences	20	46	34	565
Engineering and design	31	51	18	591
Medical and health sciences	28	50	22	681
Academic performance				
<50%	27	49	23	380
50–59%	32	45	23	1 614
60–69%	32	48	20	2 132
70%+	34	43	23	1 157
Race				
African	49	41	11	1 502
White	22	48	30	2 363
Coloured	34	46	20	1 251
Indian	27	50	24	230
Gender				
Female	32	46	22	2 955
Male	33	45	21	2 589
Language				
Afrikaans	26	46	28	1 615
English	27	49	24	2 273
African languages	49	40	10	1 464
Other languages	34	47	18	137
Age in years				
Under 22	28	47	25	3 639
22–29	41	44	15	1 667
30 or older	43	46	11	242

Black students in general and African students in particular are more frequent library users than their white counterparts. For example, 49 per cent of African students report to be frequent library users compared to 22 per cent of white students. It is important to note that 30 per cent of white students report to be infrequent library users compared to 11 per cent of African students. This is possibly due to their inability to purchase texts and a general lack of access to "own resources".

There do not seem to be any major gender differences in

patterns of library usage with 32 per cent of females reporting to be frequent library users compared to 33 per cent of males.

It is interesting to note that older students of 30 years or more (43%) report to be frequent library users than those under 22 years of age (28%).

Index of library usage by institutions and key variables

The index of library usage (Table 5.20) confirms the pattern that has emerged from the previous tables thus far. In general, library usage increases with year level. However, the big difference is that while library usage increases from the first to the postgraduate year, it declines for UWC and PT between the first and third years, and for US and CT between the third and postgraduate years. Of note is the fact that the highest proportion of frequent library users who are postgraduate students, are found at PT followed by UCT then UWC, with CT and US respectively reporting the lowest figures. Of the five institutions, US reports the lowest number of first-year students as frequent library users. It is important to note that at UCT, US and CT 25, 39 and 25 per cent of the first-year students respectively report to be infrequent users of the library, compared to 18 and nine per cent of UWC and PT first-year students respectively.

In terms of disciplinary domains across most of the institutions, humanities and social-science students report using the library more frequently than the other disciplines. At UWC economic and management science students report being frequent users of the library. However, at the technikons economic and management sciences (particularly in the case of PT) as well as engineering and design students report being frequent users of the library.

At UCT, UWC and PT more frequent users of the library (42, 40 and 52% respectively) report 70 per cent and more academic-performance scores than those in the range below 50 per cent (25, 31 and 33% respectively). This is consistent with the results of the total sample. For UCT and PT the figure of frequent library users declined between students scoring 50 to 59 per cent and those reporting 60 to 69 per cent. It is interesting to note that at US and CT there is an inverse relationship, though not significant in percentage terms, between frequent usage of the library and academic performance. For example, among US and CT students a greater proportion of frequent library users report academic performance scores of below 50 per cent (US 20%, CT 32%) than the proportion of students reporting performance scores of 70 per cent and more (US 18%, CT 27%).

Furthermore, the institutional index tables indicate that across all five institutions African students are more frequent library users than their white counterparts. This is consistent with the total sample results and suggests that it is possibly the black students who are scoring below 50 per cent at US and CT, although this cannot be confirmed.

"Of note is the fact that the highest proportion of frequent library users who are postgraduate students, are found at PT followed by UCT then UWC, with CT and US respectively reporting the lowest figures."

TABLE 5.20: Index of library usage – UCT

	Frequent use	Moderate use	Infrequent use	Total count
	Row %	Row %	Row %	
Year group				
Junior undergraduate	30	45	25	961
Senior undergraduate	40	50	10	356
Postgraduate	49	45	6	416
Disciplinary area				
Humanities	55	40	5	420
Social sciences	55	40	5	330
Economic and				
management sciences	21	47	32	411
Natural sciences	24	43	33	221
Engineering and design	—	—	—	—
Medical and health sciences	23	62	15	349
Academic performance				
<50%	25	45	30	88
50–59%	35	46	19	334
60–69%	34	49	17	757
70%+	42	43	15	474
Race				
African	49	40	11	416
White	30	49	22	908
Coloured	43	43	13	226
Indian	31	53	16	116
Gender				
Female	38	47	15	934
Male	36	45	19	793
Language				
Afrikaans	48	41	11	73
English	31	49	20	1 154
African languages	51	39	10	387
Other languages	35	48	17	100
Age in years				
Under 22	31	48	22	1 173
22–29	48	44	8	509
30 or older	54	42	4	48

At US, UWC and PT, more males than females report to be frequent users of the library. At UCT and PT the results indicate that more females than males are frequent library users.

The institutional tables indicate that older students (30+) are more frequent library users than the younger group (<22). This is consistent with the pattern reflected in the table for the total sample. The highest number of frequent library users for the age.

A striking finding of the results of the index of library usage is the fact that African students report to be frequent library users.

TABLE 5.21: Index of library usage – US

	Frequent use	Moderate use	Infrequent use	Total count
	Row %	Row %	Row %	
Year group				
Junior undergraduate	16	45	39	921
Senior undergraduate	29	55	16	181
Postgraduate	24	43	34	185
Disciplinary area				
Humanities	27	49	24	204
Social sciences	25	41	33	332
Economic and management sciences	14	51	34	457
Natural sciences	14	42	44	185
Engineering and design	—	—	—	—
Medical and health sciences	13	44	43	111
Academic performance				
<50%	20	46	34	90
50–59%	19	46	35	362
60–69%	18	50	31	505
70%+	18	41	41	296
Race				
African	27	59	14	22
White	16	47	37	1 076
Coloured	36	41	23	162
Indian	50	25	25	8
Gender				
Female	18	44	38	789
Male	21	49	30	498
Language				
Afrikaans	19	45	36	840
English	19	48	33	389
African languages	30	65	5	20
Other languages	22	39	39	18
Age in years				
Under 22	18	45	36	1 065
22–29	22	51	27	192
30 or older	27	50	23	30

The pattern that emerges for the group African by institution is the following: 55 per cent of the proportion of PT students, 49 per cent of the proportion of students at UCT, 47 per cent of the proportion of students for CT, 47 per cent of the proportion of students for UWC and 27 per cent of the proportion of students for US. The number of frequent African library users in the total sample was 49 per cent. This, as the focus-group interviews pointed out, is perhaps due to the socio-economic background of students, with

TABLE 5.22: Index of library usage — UWC

	Frequent use	Moderate use	Infrequent use	Total count
	Row %	Row %	Row %	
Year group				
Junior undergraduate	38	44	18	555
Senior undergraduate	34	45	20	473
Postgraduate	45	37	18	211
Disciplinary area				
Humanities	50	40	10	308
Social sciences	23	55	22	159
Economic and management sciences	30	44	26	370
Natural sciences	23	55	22	159
Engineering and design	—	—	—	—
Medical and health sciences	27	31	43	49
Academic performance				
<50%	31	52	18	95
50–59%	34	44	22	528
60–69%	41	45	14	409
70%+	40	36	24	138
Race				
African	47	40	13	631
White	25	63	13	8
Coloured	29	46	25	447
Indian	19	46	35	98
Gender				
Female	36	45	18	693
Male	40	40	20	538
Language				
Afrikaans	32	47	21	243
English	25	46	30	340
African languages	47	40	13	625
Other languages	40	60	—	5
Age in years				
Under 22	32	46	22	590
22–29	42	40	18	549
30 or older	47	42	11	91

African students requiring the library in terms of spatial and information resources while more white students have access to other resources such as study space.

Two other features of the results are important to note. Firstly, there seems to be a strong relationship between reported academic-performance scores and frequent usage of the library in three of the institutions, namely UCT, UWC and PT. It is unclear why this is not the case at US and PT. Secondly, it is also convincingly the

TABLE 5.23: Index of library usage — CT

	Frequent use	Moderate use	Infrequent use	Total count
	Row %	Row %	Row %	
Year group				
Junior undergraduate	28	48	25	407
Senior undergraduate	31	56	13	120
Postgraduate	27	54	19	95
Disciplinary area				
Humanities	—	—	—	—
Social sciences	41	51	8	61
Economic and management sciences	25	50	26	155
Natural sciences	—	—	—	—
Engineering and design	26	53	21	314
Medical and health sciences	—	—	—	—
Academic performance				
<50%	32	47	21	47
50–59%	28	51	21	166
60–69%	29	48	23	236
70%+	27	52	21	154
Race				
African	46	44	10	115
White	23	51	26	363
Coloured	27	50	24	123
Indian	29	57	14	7
Gender				
Female	35	50	15	234
Male	24	51	26	386
Language				
Afrikaans	25	47	28	235
English	22	55	22	264
African languages	47	44	9	109
Other languages	36	55	9	11
Age in years				
Under 22	27	49	24	426
22–29	32	51	18	146
30 or older	32	56	12	50

case that older students are more frequent library users. Whether maturity is an aspect of library usage is an issue that requires further investigation.

Index of information needs

One of the main objectives of the survey was to establish what the main information needs of the students at the five higher-

TABLE 5.24: Index of library usage – PT

	Frequent use	Moderate use	Infrequent use	Total count
	Row %	Row %	Row %	
Year group				
Junior undergraduate	49	42	9	393
Senior undergraduate	38	50	12	217
Postgraduate	52	36	12	73
Disciplinary area				
Humanities	—	—	—	—
Social sciences	49	41	10	178
Economic and management sciences	54	40	6	89
Natural sciences	—	—	—	—
Engineering and design	37	49	14	277
Medical and health sciences	53	39	8	136
Academic performance				
<50%	33	58	8	60
50–59%	45	44	11	224
60–69%	41	46	13	225
70%+	52	40	8	95
Race				
African	55	39	6	318
White	13	50	38	8
Coloured	37	49	14	293
Indian	—	100	—	1
Gender				
Female	44	46	11	305
Male	47	43	10	374
Language				
Afrikaans	41	49	10	224
English	29	48	22	126
African languages	54	39	7	323
Other languages	67	33	—	3
Age in years				
Under 22	44	44	12	385
22–29	46	44	10	271
30 or older	52	43	4	23

education institutions are. Eleven items (Q4.31 to 4.41) were included in the questionnaire to measure such needs.

An initial factor analysis revealed an optimal solution into three factors explaining 68 per cent of the variance. The three-factor solution clustered items 4.31 to 4.34 , 4.35 to 4.37 and 4.38 to 4.41 together. The interpretation of this solution suggests that the more standard information and library needs constitute one factor (items 4.31 to 4.34), with the specifically computer-related needs separated into more basic computer needs (word-processing, spreadsheets and database) on the one hand and more advanced computer needs (graphics, statistical analysis, CAD and the Internet) on the other.

On this basis three different information needs indices were constructed:

- Index of basic information needs,
- Index of basic computer-related needs and
- Index of advanced computer-related needs

Similar procedures were followed as before. The resultant distribution of scores are presented in Charts 5.5, 5.6 and 5.7 below.

In general, if the first two categories of graph 11 (high need and moderate need) are combined, approximately 60 per cent of the proportion of students in the sample fall into these categories. UWC and PT also report the lowest proportion of students in the

CHART 5.5: Frequency count of the index of basic information needs in the region

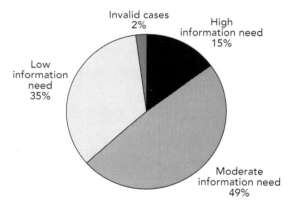

CHART 5.6: Frequency count of the index of basic computer-related information needs

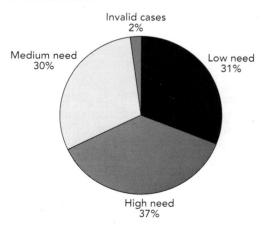

**CHART 5.7: Frequency count of the index of advanced computer-related
information needs**

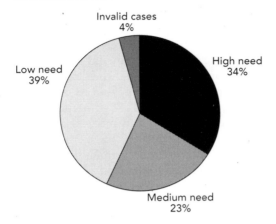

GRAPH 5.5: Institutional results of the index of basic information needs across the region

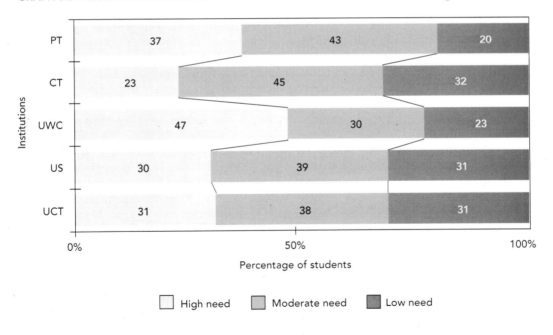

low-need category. This implies the need for training in basic
information needs across the region.

Index of basic information needs of the total sample

Table 5.25 indicates that for the total sample the number of students in the high-need category declines from the undergraduate
to the postgraduate levels (first year: 16% of the proportion of
students; third year: 16% of the proportion of students; postgraduate: 11% of the proportion of students). Lowest-need-

category figures increase across year levels so that postgraduate students report a higher incidence of lowest need (43%) than junior and senior undergraduate students (each 34%). Basic information needs decrease from undergraduate to postgraduate levels.

The index of basic information needs reveals interesting patterns in respect of disciplinary domain. Table 31 indicates that it is students in the humanities (18%) and social sciences (18%) domains who report high need compared to students in the economics and management sciences (15%), natural sciences (11%), engineering and design (12%), and medical and health sciences (12%).

Table 5.25 indicates also that there is a strong relationship between basic information needs and academic performance. Thus, students who do not report high scores report high need. The results indicate that frequent library users score better and record low basic-information needs. In other words, these students are actively and successfully addressing their basic information needs.

A greater proportion of black students falls into the high-need category than their white counterparts. This pattern is similar to that obtained from the index of library usage but suggests that, while more black students address their information needs, they still experience high levels of basic information needs.

Gender analysis indicates that a greater proportion of female students (16%) report to be in the high-need category than males (10%), again underscoring their greater levels of need as in other indices.

"... frequent library users score better and record low basic-information needs."

Analysis by age group indicates that more older students report high need than younger students (30+: 19% as opposed to <22: 14%). Conversely, fewer older students (25%) report low levels of need than younger students (37%). Thus, it is the mature students who report higher need than the other two groups. There is thus a strong relationship between high information needs and increase in age.

Index of basic information needs by institutions and key variables

Tables 5.26 to 5.30 provide a profile of the index of basic information needs for each institution. In respect of basic information needs, the tables indicate that in four of the five institutions students in the postgraduate (4th year) group, appear less frequently in the high-need category than those in the first year. However, this picture is slightly different for CT where students in the postgraduate cohort (16%) fall much more in the high-need category than the first-year group (10%). Furthermore, at UCT, third-year students (5%) fall less in the high-need category than the postgraduate group (6%), though in this case the difference is marginal in percentage terms.

TABLE 5.25: Index of basic information needs – Total sample

	High-need category Row %	Moderate-need category Row %	Lowest need category Row %	Total count
Year group				
Junior undergraduate	16	51	34	3 207
Senior undergraduate	16	50	34	1 344
Postgraduate	11	46	43	978
Disciplinary area				
Humanities	18	48	34	924
Social sciences	18	52	30	1 254
Economic and management sciences	15	49	36	1 463
Natural sciences	11	50	39	561
Engineering and design	12	51	37	589
Medical and health sciences	12	47	41	679
Academic performance				
<50%	20	56	24	374
50–59%	19	53	28	1 604
60–69%	14	49	36	222
70%+	10	43	47	1 155
Race				
African	23	56	21	1 481
White	8	45	47	2 360
Coloured	19	53	28	1 247
Indian	14	49	36	222
Gender				
Female	16	50	34	1 617
Male	10	45	45	2 257
Language				
Afrikaans	14	52	34	1 617
English	10	45	45	2 257
African languages	24	55	21	1 444
Other languages	12	50	38	136
Age in years				
Under 22	14	49	37	3 613
22–29	17	50	33	1 658
30 or older	19	56	25	243

Basic information needs also differ across disciplinary domains. At UCT more students in the natural sciences, engineering and design disciplinary domains are more often in the high-need category than other disciplines, though the difference is only about one to two per cent in most cases. Thus, the picture is fairly even for most of the disciplinary domains at UCT. At US the pattern that emerges is that it is students in the humanities (15%) and social sciences (16%) who are in the high-need category compared to, for example, those in the natural sciences (8%). Again, at

UWC it is students in the humanities and social sciences who report the high-need category compared to the other disciplinary domains. The picture at CT is fairly even with about ten per cent reporting in the high-need category. The deviation is in the economic and management sciences where there are 14 per cent students in the high-need category. At PT, economic and management science students are the majority in the high-need category (28%). Given this picture, it is difficult to draw firm generalisations across disciplinary domains.

In respect of reported academic performance, there is a clear pattern between students in the range below 50 per cent and those with scores of 70 per cent. A greater proportion of students who record scores of less than 50 per cent fall in the high-need category than those with scores of 70 per cent. For example, at UCT, 29 per cent of students who score below 50 per cent are in the high-need category compared to five per cent of those reporting performance scores of 70 per cent. The interesting feature though is at US, UWC and CT where there does not seem to be an obvious correlation between high need and scores of 50 to 59 and 60 to 69 per cent. At US, 11 per cent of students who score 50 to 59 per cent fall in the high-need category, compared to 12 per cent of those reporting 60 to 69 per cent. At UWC, 27 per cent of students who score 50 to 59 per cent fall in the high-need category, compared to 26 per cent of those reporting 60 to 69 per cent. At CT, ten per cent of students who score 50 to 59 per cent fall in the high-need category compared to 15 per cent of those reporting 60 to 69 per cent. In essence, the results suggest that students with scores of 70 per cent report less need, indicating a strong relationship between performance and basic information needs.

> *"Of note is the fact that at all institutions, barring CT, there are more older students (30+) in the high-need category than those aged below 22."*

Without exception, at all of the five institutions a greater proportion of black students in general and African in particular fall in the high-need category than their white counterparts. At the five institutions the proportion of African students is as follows: UCT 18 per cent (white 5%), US 23 per cent (white 9%), UWC 29 per cent and PT 23%.[3]

A greater proportion of female students fall in the high-need category than males: at UCT (female 10%, male 9%), US (female 13%, male 8%), CT (female 15%, male 9%) and PT (female 23%, male 16%). This pattern is consistent with that revealed in the results for the total sample. It is interesting to note the significant differences at US and CT. It is only at UWC that less females record scores in this category, though only marginally so (female 25%, male 26%).

Of note is the fact that at all institutions, barring CT, there are more older students (30+) in the high-need category than those aged below 22. The one interesting feature is the variance across the age groups. There does not seem to be a steady increase in students in the high-need category across all age level. Thus, at UCT, the age range 22 to 29 reports the lowest high-need group

TABLE 5.26: Index of basic information needs – UCT

	High-need category	Moderate-need category	Lowest need category	Total count
	Row %	Row %	Row %	
Year group				
Junior undergraduate	13	44	43	953
Senior undergraduate	5	46	49	354
Postgraduate	6	40	54	411
Disciplinary area				
Humanities	8	45	47	326
Social sciences	10	42	48	407
Economic and				
management sciences	9	47	44	220
Natural sciences	11	41	48	346
Engineering and design	—	—	—	—
Medical and health sciences	11	41	48	346
Academic performance				
<50%	29	44	27	86
50–59%	16	50	34	331
60–69%	8	45	48	750
70%+	5	36	59	473
Race				
African	18	54	28	406
White	5	38	57	906
Coloured	14	48	38	225
Indian	11	45	44	114
Gender				
Female	10	44	46	927
Male	9	43	48	785
Language				
Afrikaans	11	44	45	73
English	7	40	53	1 150
African languages	19	54	28	377
Other languages	12	45	42	99
Age in years				
Under 22	11	43	47	1 165
22–29	8	45	47	502
30 or older	13	52	35	48

(8%) for the institution. This is also the case at US (7%). At UWC, the age group 22 to 29 reports the greatest high need (29%) for the institution. At CT, both the age group below 22 and those 22 to 29 years of age report the same proportion in the high-need category (12%) for the institution. At PT the age group 22 to 29 reports the lowest high-need category for the institution.

In general, if the first two categories of Tables 5.26 to 5.30 are combined (high need and moderate need), approximately 60 per cent of students fall into these categories.

TABLE 5.27: Index of basic information needs – US

	High-need category	Moderate-need category	Lowest need category	Total count
	Row %	Row %	Row %	
Year group				
Junior undergraduate	13	51	36	919
Senior undergraduate	10	47	43	182
Postgraduate	5	49	46	186
Disciplinary area				
Humanities	15	50	35	202
Social sciences	16	51	33	334
Economic and management sciences	9	51	40	457
Natural sciences	8	48	44	185
Engineering and design	—	—	—	—
Medical and health sciences	5	50	45	111
Academic performance				
<50%	14	52	33	90
50–59%	11	53	36	363
60–69%	12	49	39	503
70%+	9	50	42	296
Race				
African	23	45	32	22
White	9	50	41	1 074
Coloured	23	49	28	163
Indian	13	50	38	8
Gender				
Female	13	50	37	788
Male	8	51	41	499
Language				
Afrikaans	12	49	39	843
English	8	52	39	387
African languages	25	45	30	20
Other languages	6	71	24	17
Age in years				
Under 22	12	51	37	1 064
22–29	7	47	47	193
30 or older	17	50	33	30

Two other features of the index of basic information needs are worth noting. Firstly, there is a strong relationship between reported academic performance and those students in the high-need category. It is thus the case that the better performer requires less help. Secondly, that at all five institutions a greater proportion of black students, and African students in particular, fall in the high-need category.

TABLE 5.28: Index of basic information needs – UWC

	High-need category Row %	Moderate-need category Row %	Lowest need category Row %	Total count
Year group				
Junior undergraduate	27	56	17	535
Senior undergraduate	26	51	23	472
Postgraduate	23	51	26	211
Disciplinary area				
Humanities	30	52	17	305
Social sciences	28	52	20	352
Economic and				
management sciences	25	54	22	355
Natural sciences	18	55	27	156
Engineering and design	—	—	—	—
Medical and health sciences	14	53	33	49
Academic performance				
<50%	25	59	15	91
50–59%	27	53	20	519
60–69%	26	54	21	402
70%+	19	51	29	136
Race				
African	29	54	18	620
White	25	75	—	8
Coloured	22	54	24	442
Indian	18	54	28	93
Gender				
Female	25	54	21	680
Male	26	52	21	530
Language				
Afrikaans	23	58	19	242
English	20	51	29	330
African languages	30	53	17	615
Other languages	—	100	—	5
Age in years				
Under 22	23	54	23	575
22–29	29	52	19	544
30 or older	26	57	16	91

Index of basic computer-related needs across institutions in the region

Graph 5.6 (p.128) provides a regional profile of basic computer-related needs by institution. It is evident that the HDIs express highest levels of basic computer-related needs with 47 and 37 per cent of the proportion of students at UWC and PT respectively reporting high levels of computer-related needs, compared to 31 per cent of UCT's students, 30 per cent at US and 23 per cent at CT. They also report the least cases of low-level needs in this index

TABLE 5.29: Index of basic information needs – CT

	High-need category	Moderate-need category	Lowest need category	Total count
	Row %	Row %	Row %	
Year group				
Junior undergraduate	10	54	36	407
Senior undergraduate	13	47	40	119
Postgraduate	16	42	42	95
Disciplinary area				
Humanities	—	—	—	—
Social sciences	11	66	23	62
Economic and management sciences	14	54	33	155
Natural sciences	—	—	—	—
Engineering and design	9	47	44	313
Medical and health sciences	11	56	33	36
Academic performance				
<50%	13	64	22	114
50–59%	10	46	45	364
60–69%	15	54	31	123
70%+	17	50	33	6
Race				
African	14	64	22	114
White	10	46	45	364
Coloured	15	54	31	123
Indian	17	50	33	6
Gender				
Female	15	51	34	234
Male	9	50	40	385
Language				
Afrikaans	12	49	38	234
English	11	47	43	264
African languages	13	65	22	109
Other languages	9	50	40	385
Age in years				
Under 22	12	52	37	425
22–29	12	45	43	147
30 or older	10	59	31	49

(23 and 20 per cent of their proportions of students respectively). Not surprisingly, CT, which is the most advanced IT institution in terms of student access to and use of computer applications, reports only 23 per cent of their proportion of students in the high-need category.

Of concern is the fact that 73 per cent of the proportion of students in the sample express a high or moderate need for basic computer skills. This picture is highlighted by the fact, suggested by that table, that on average 33 per cent of the total sample of students are in the high-need category.

TABLE 5.30: Index of basic information needs — PT

	High-need category	Moderate-need category	Lowest need category	Total count
	Row %	Row %	Row %	
Year group				
Junior undergraduate	20	54	26	393
Senior undergraduate	19	59	22	217
Postgraduate	16	63	21	75
Disciplinary area				
Humanities	—	—	—	—
Social sciences	20	61	19	180
Economic and management sciences	28	55	17	89
Natural sciences	—	—	—	—
Engineering and design	15	55	29	276
Medical and health sciences	20	53	27	137
Academic performance				
<50%	14	66	20	59
50–59%	19	56	25	226
60–69%	19	54	27	226
70%+	22	54	24	95
Race				
African	23	58	18	319
White	—	63	38	8
Coloured	16	56	28	294
Indian	—	100	—	1
Gender				
Female	23	54	23	307
Male	16	59	25	374
Language				
Afrikaans	16	60	24	225
English	14	48	37	126
African languages	23	58	20	323
Other languages	50	50	—	4
Age in years				
Under 22	20	54	27	384
22–29	18	60	22	272
30 or older	20	64	16	25

Index of basic computer-related needs of the total sample

Table 5.31 indicates that across year levels for the total sample, it is the third-year students (38 per cent) who express the greatest need for basic computer skills, followed by postgraduate students (34%) and then first-years (32%). This possibly suggests that students entering university are more familiar with computer-based applications.

In respect of disciplinary domains, students in the humanities (41%) and social sciences (35%) express greater need for basic computer skills than the other disciplines. It is important to note

GRAPH 5.6: Institutional results of the index of basic computer-related needs across the region

	High need	Moderate need	Low need
PT	37	43	20
CT	23	45	32
UWC	47	30	23
US	30	39	31
UCT	31	38	31

Institutions (y-axis)
Percentage of students (x-axis): 0%, 50%, 100%

☐ High need   ▨ Moderate need   ■ Low need

that the largest proportion of students in the high-need category are found in the domain of engineering and design (24%), a domain that is exclusively specific to the technikons in this investigation. This suggests that at the technikons, in the engineering and design domain, there is greater computer activity and awareness.

The results by academic performance indicate that there is some relationship between high-need and reported academic performance scores. Thus, the least number of students (30%) in the high-need category report scores of 70 per cent. However, this does not apply uniformly to all the other scores. Students below 50 per cent (32%) fall less in the high-need category than those with scores of 50 to 59 per cent (36%) and 60 to 69 per cent (34%). It is important to note that the percentage differences between the scores are in many cases small.

Table 5.31 also indicates that black students in general are the majority in the high-need category. The breakdown reveals that among black students, more Indian (47%) students, followed by coloured (43%) and then African students (38%), express high need. This contrasts the white student figure of 25 per cent.

The gender breakdown reveals that a greater proportion of females (37%) than males (33%) fall in the high basic-computer-information needs category.

With regard to age, there are no large differences as far as basic computer-related needs are concerned, with the age group 22 to 29 years recording the highest proportion of students in the high-need category (36%).

TABLE 5.31: Index of basic computer-related needs – Total sample

	High-need category	Moderate-need category	Lowest need category	Total count
	Row %	Row %	Row %	
Year group				
Junior undergraduate	32	38	29	3 187
Senior undergraduate	38	37	26	1 342
Postgraduate	34	38	28	977
Disciplinary area				
Humanities	41	31	28	920
Social sciences	35	38	26	1 250
Economic and management sciences	32	40	28	1 455
Natural sciences	33	40	27	558
Engineering and design	24	43	33	587
Medical and health sciences	36	35	29	677
Academic performance				
<50%	32	43	26	371
50–59%	36	38	26	1 597
60–69%	34	38	28	2 109
70%+	30	38	32	1 152
Race				
African	38	36	26	1 471
White	25	40	35	2 356
Coloured	43	37	20	1 239
Indian	47	36	17	222
Gender				
Female	37	38	25	1 610
Male	33	38	29	2 252
Language				
Afrikaans	33	39	28	1 610
English	33	38	29	2 252
African languages	38	37	26	1 435
Other languages	27	35	38	134
Age in years				
Under 22	33	39	28	3 596
22–29	36	36	28	1 562
30 or older	29	42	29	243

Index of basic computer-related needs by institutions and key variables

Tables 5.32 to 5.36 below provide the results for basic computer-related needs for each institution. The tables suggest that the proportion of UCT, US and PT students in the high-need category declines across the three year levels. Thus, postgraduate students express a lesser need for basic computer-related training than those in the first year. At UWC the pattern reverses with more postgraduate students (54%) in the high-need category than first-years

(37%). At CT, while there are more postgraduate students (26%) in the high-need category compared to first-years (23%), the lowest number of students in the high-need category are third-years (21%), though the difference is small.

In the case of disciplinary domains, students at UCT, US and CT in the high-need category were those in humanities and social sciences, confirming the expectation that information technologies are less widespread in these areas. Thus, at UCT (35%), US (45%) and CT (44%) humanities and social science students were in the high-need category. At UCT the lowest percentage for high need for disciplinary domain was economic and management sciences; medical sciences at US, engineering and design at CT. At UWC and PT the picture that emerges is that in all disciplines there were significant numbers of students (30 to 40%) in the high-need category. This situation was most marked at UWC with more than 45 per cent of the students in the high-need category. The interesting feature of UWC is that it was the natural sciences and the economic and management sciences that expressed high need. It is thus the case that at UWC and PT students expressed high need for basic computer-related training and skills.

With respect to reported academic performance, at UCT and CT students reporting high scores report less high need than those with low scores. Thus, across the various score levels, at these two institutions high need is inversely related to reported performance. At US, UWC and PT the picture is that high need is directly related to performance. Thus, students reporting scores of 70 per cent at the three institutions also expressed high need for basic computer-related training and skills.

"The correlation between age and the basic computer-related needs displays marked variation across the five institutions."

Figures by race are again not surprising. Across the region, the results indicate that there are more black students in the high-need category than there are white students. With regard to black students, the results indicate that of the five institutions, there are more coloured students in the high-need category than African students, with the exception of CT.

A gender breakdown indicates that at four of the institutions, UCT (female 34%, male 27%), US (female 35%, male 22%), UWC (female 47%, male 46%) and CT (female 33%, male 17%) more females are found in the high-need category than their male counterparts. The most significant difference is at CT where about twice as many females as males are in the high-need category. By contrast, at PT (female 34%, male 38%) there are more males than females in the high-need category.

The correlation between age and the basic computer-related needs displays marked variation across the five institutions. At the three universities, the age of students appears in inverse relation to high computer-related need. Thus, there are fewer students aged 30 years and older in the high-need category at the three universities than those aged below 22. At CT and PT, there are more students aged 30 years and older in the high-need category than those aged

TABLE 5.32: Index of basic computer-related needs – UCT

	High-need category	Moderate-need category	Lowest need category	Total count
	Row %	Row %	Row %	
Year group				
Junior undergraduate	32	37	31	946
Senior undergraduate	28	39	34	352
Postgraduate	31	41	28	411
Disciplinary area				
Humanities	35	34	32	415
Social sciences	32	43	25	325
Economic and management sciences	23	40	37	404
Natural sciences	32	41	27	219
Engineering and design	—	—	—	—
Medical and health sciences	33	35	32	344
Academic performance				
<50%	38	40	22	86
50–59%	34	41	26	328
60–69%	33	37	31	746
70%+	25	37	37	472
Race				
African	39	35	25	401
White	24	39	37	905
Coloured	42	35	23	222
Indian	41	41	18	114
Gender				
Female	34	39	27	924
Male	27	37	36	779
Language				
Afrikaans	29	40	31	72
English	28	39	32	1 148
African languages	39	37	24	372
Other languages	28	33	40	98
Age in years				
Under 22	32	38	31	1 159
22–29	29	38	32	499
30 or older	29	52	19	48

younger than 22. In fact, the CT results indicate that age is in inverse relation to the category of high need.

The institutional comparative analysis confirms most of the features obtained for the sample as a whole. Three key features of the index of computer-related needs are worth noting. First, a high proportion of students across all institutions express high/ moderate need for computer-related training. Secondly, black students in general express high need for computer-related training. Thirdly, UWC and PT tend to have a higher proportion of students in the high-need category.

TABLE 5.33: Index of basic computer-related needs – US

	High-need category	Moderate-need category	Lowest need category	Total count
	Row %	Row %	Row %	
Year group				
Junior undergraduate	31	39	30	916
Senior undergraduate	31	38	30	182
Postgraduate	24	39	37	186
Disciplinary area				
Humanities	45	31	23	201
Social sciences	31	38	31	333
Economic and management sciences	27	41	32	456
Natural sciences	24	46	29	185
Engineering and design	—	—	—	—
Medical and health sciences	23	33	44	111
Academic performance				
<50%	27	46	27	89
50–59%	29	39	32	362
60–69%	30	39	31	502
70%+	31	38	31	296
Race				
African	36	41	23	22
White	29	39	32	1 072
Coloured	36	39	25	162
Indian	25	50	25	8
Gender				
Female	35	37	28	786
Male	22	42	35	498
Language				
Afrikaans	30	38	33	840
English	31	41	28	387
African languages	30	40	30	20
Other languages	24	47	29	17
Age in years				
Under 22	31	40	29	1 061
22–29	28	31	41	193
30 or older	17	47	37	30

Index of advanced computer-related needs across institutions in the region

Graph 5.7 (see p.136) below confirms the pattern of large differences between the HDIs and HAIs. Students at UWC and PT report the highest need for advanced computer-related training (43 and 46% of the proportions of students in their samples respectively). Interestingly, students at CT, where IT awareness and practices are advanced, report a fairly high level of need (34% of their proportions of students in their sample) in comparison to

TABLE 5.34: Index of basic computer-related needs – UWC

	High-need category	Moderate-need category	Lowest need category	Total count
	Row %	Row %	Row %	
Year group				
Junior undergraduate	37	31	32	529
Senior undergraduate	54	30	17	472
Postgraduate	54	27	18	211
Disciplinary area				
Humanities	46	26	27	304
Social sciences	43	29	28	352
Economic and management sciences	50	35	15	352
Natural sciences	45	31	24	154
Engineering and design	—	—	—	—
Medical and health sciences	55	20	24	49
Academic performance				
<50%	30	42	28	89
50–59%	46	29	25	516
60–69%	49	30	21	302
70%+	53	28	19	136
Race				
African	40	30	30	616
White	38	38	25	8
Coloured	53	31	16	440
Indian	57	29	14	93
Gender				
Female	47	30	23	677
Male	46	31	24	527
Language				
Afrikaans	54	31	15	241
English	54	29	17	329
African languages	40	30	30	612
Other languages	75	25	—	4
Age in years				
Under 22	48	29	23	571
22–29	48	29	23	542
30 or older	31	41	29	91

students at UCT (27%) and US (22%). This presumably results from a greater awareness of gaps and needs at this institution and puts CT on par with UWC and PT in respect of the low-need category (CT 31%; UWC 34% and PT 30% of the proportion of students). These results correspond closely to the pattern of access to facilities among the HDIs and reports of need at these institutions.

If the figures for "high-need" and "moderate-need" categories are combined, the regional picture which emerges is that only 36 per cent of the proportion of students report in the "low-need"

TABLE 5.35: Index of basic computer-related needs – CT

	High-need category	Moderate-need category	Lowest need category	Total count
	Row %	Row %	Row %	
Year group				
Junior undergraduate	23	48	30	404
Senior undergraduate	21	42	37	119
Postgraduate	26	37	37	95
Disciplinary area				
Humanities	—	—	—	—
Social sciences	44	44	11	61
Economic and management sciences	23	54	23	155
Natural sciences	—	—	—	—
Engineering and design	15	41	43	311
Medical and health sciences	42	35	22	36
Academic performance				
<50%	33	46	21	48
50–59%	24	45	32	165
60–69%	22	46	33	235
70%+	20	44	35	153
Race				
African	34	46	20	113
White	18	44	38	363
Coloured	28	47	25	235
Indian	33	33	33	153
Gender				
Female	33	47	20	233
Male	17	43	40	383
Language				
Afrikaans	20	44	37	234
English	23	44	32	262
African languages	31	51	18	108
Other languages	—	36	64	11
Age in years				
Under 22	22	45	33	422
22–29	26	44	30	147
30 or older	27	41	33	49

category while 64 per cent of students claim a moderate or high degree of advanced computer-related information needs.

Index of advanced computer-related needs of the total sample

Table 5.37 (p.137) indicates that for year groups it is the third year sample that expresses the greatest need (37%) for advanced computer-related training. The first-year- and postgraduate-

TABLE 5.36: Index of basic computer-related needs – PT

	High-need category	Moderate-need category	Lowest need category	Total count
	Row %	Row %	Row %	
Year group				
Junior undergraduate	40	41	20	392
Senior undergraduate	34	44	22	217
Postgraduate	28	54	18	74
Disciplinary area				
Humanities	—	—	—	—
Social sciences	32	46	22	179
Economic and				
management sciences	42	32	26	88
Natural sciences	—	—	—	—
Engineering and design	35	45	21	276
Medical and health sciences	43	43	14	137
Academic performance				
<50%	29	41	31	59
50–59%	35	47	18	226
60–69%	37	43	20	224
70%+	37	42	21	95
Race				
African	33	46	21	319
White	25	50	25	8
Coloured	39	43	18	293
Indian	—	—	100	1
Gender				
Female	34	46	19	306
Male	38	40	21	373
Language				
Afrikaans	38	45	17	223
English	40	35	25	126
African languages	34	45	21	323
Other languages	50	50	—	4
Age in years				
Under 22	37	44	19	383
22–29	35	44	21	271
30 or older	40	28	32	25

sample results are equal in respect of students who are in the high-need category (31%).

The results for disciplinary domain reflect a fairly even high-need category for the entire sample. The one significant feature is engineering and design for which as many as 44 per cent of the sample express a high need for advanced computer-related training where presumably these skills are required most.

With respect to performance, there is a clear decline between

GRAPH 5.7: Institutional results of the index of advanced computer-related needs

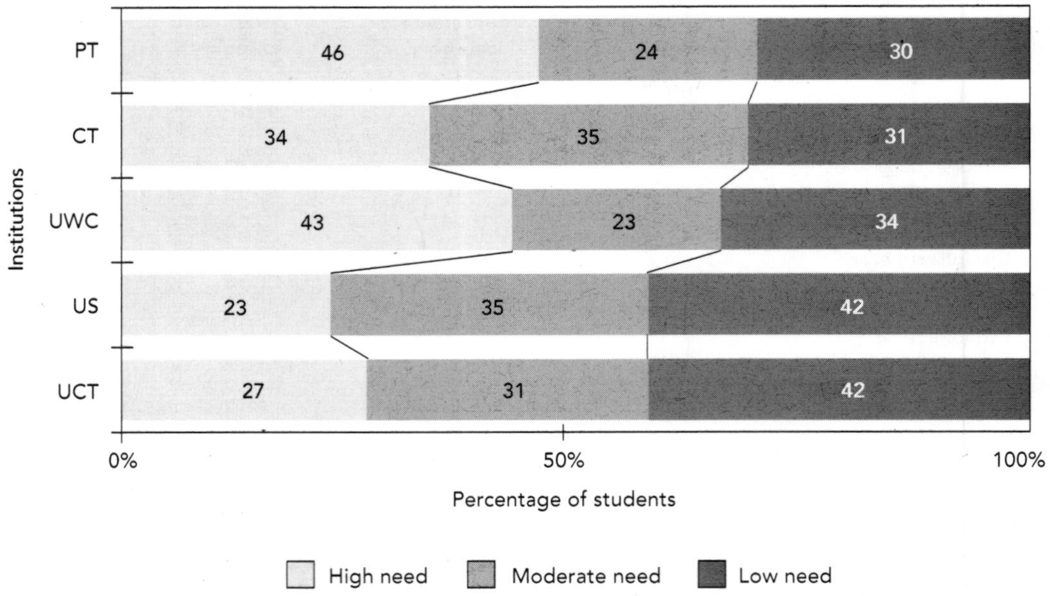

Institution	High need	Moderate need	Low need
PT	46	24	30
CT	34	35	31
UWC	43	23	34
US	23	35	42
UCT	27	31	42

Percentage of students

☐ High need   ▨ Moderate need   ■ Low need

high need for advanced computer-related training of students reporting scores of 70 per cent and more (28%), compared to those with scores of less than 50 per cent (31%). The interesting feature is scores of 50 to 59 per cent and 60 to 69 per cent, where 33 per cent of the sample express a high need for advanced computer-related training.

Black students in general (African 28% of the proportion of the sample, coloured 42% of the proportion of the sample and Indian 45% of the proportion of the sample) express a greater need for advanced computer-related training than their white counterparts (21% of the proportion of the sample). It is important to note that in this specific instance it is Indian and coloured students who express a high need compared to African students.

The gender breakdown does not reveal any important difference in the total sample, with 32 per cent of females expressing a high need for advanced computer-related training compared to 33 per cent of males. However, of note is the fact that more males express high need for this training. This is in contradistinction to basic computer-related training where more females than males express high need.

The results for age is similar to year-group analysis. Thus, more third-year students (35%) express a high need for advanced computer-related training compared to first-years and postgraduates (both 31%).

TABLE 5.37: Index of advanced computer-related needs – Total sample

	High-need category	Moderate-need category	Low-need category	Total count
	Row %	Row %	Row %	
Year group				
Junior undergraduate	31	31	38	3 134
Senior undergraduate	37	29	34	1 336
Postgraduate	31	29	40	963
Disciplinary area				
Humanities	31	26	43	899
Social sciences	30	27	43	1 234
Economic and management sciences	33	34	33	1 437
Natural sciences	30	35	35	554
Engineering and design	44	30	27	584
Medical and health sciences	29	28	43	669
Academic performance				
<50%	31	28	41	364
50–59%	33	30	36	1 568
60–69%	33	29	38	2 087
70%+	28	34	38	1 145
Race				
African	38	22	40	1 431
White	21	36	43	2 340
Coloured	42	29	29	1 226
Indian	45	27	28	221
Gender				
Female	32	28	40	2 889
Male	33	32	35	2 526
Language				
Afrikaans	29	33	37	1 592
English	31	32	37	2 239
African languages	39	22	39	1 397
Other languages	28	30	42	131
Age in years				
Under 22	31	31	37	3 555
22–29	35	27	38	1 633
30 or older	31	31	39	232

Index of advanced computer-related needs by institutions and key variables

The institutional index analysis indicates that for year groups at UCT and US there are fewer postgraduate students who express high need for advanced computer-related training than first-year students. However, at UCT it is the third-year group (23%) who of all year groups have the lowest figure in the high-need category. At US, there is an increase from first- (22%) to third-year (24%) figures but a decline from third year to the postgraduate period

(20%). At UWC, across all the year levels, the number of students in the high-need category increases. The results for the two technikons indicate an inverse relation between year level and high need. Thus, at both technikons fewer postgraduate students are in the high-need category than compared to first-years. It is possibly the case that students at the technikons are more familiar with advanced computer-related applications in their final year as opposed to their beginning year.

The results for disciplinary domains reveal wide differences among and within the five institutions. If one only considers the results for the disciplinary domains with the greater proportion of students expressing high need, the picture that emerges is the following: UCT = natural sciences, US = humanities, UWC = medical and health sciences, CT = humanities and social sciences and PT = engineering design. This is an interesting result and one that requires more careful consideration, since it suggests that at the three HAIs humanities and social sciences students need the most advanced computer skills, while students in the applied disciplines at the HDIs need them. However, caution should be exercised in interpreting this result, as the difference between domains by institutions is not large in percentage terms.

With regard to academic performance, at UCT, US and CT the results indicate that students who report scores of 70 per cent and more express a lesser need for advanced computer-related training than those with scores below 50 per cent. There is no clear pattern at these three institutions between high need and students reporting scores of 50 to 59 per cent and 60 to 69 per cent. At UWC and PT it is significant to note that there is a direct relationship between performance scores and the high-need category. Thus, students in the higher-mark ranges (60 to 69% and 70%) express a greater need for advanced computer-related training as opposed to students in the other ranges. This implies that for UWC and PT there is a strong correlation between the high need for training and reported academic performance.

Across all five institutions, the results indicate that black students in general express a high need for advanced computer-related training. AT UCT, 36 per cent African and coloured students and 44 per cent Indian students express a high need for advanced computer-related training as opposed to 18 per cent white students. At US, 27 per cent African and 33 per cent coloured students express a high need for advanced computer-related training as opposed to 20 per cent white students. At UWC, 38 per cent African, 46 per cent coloured and 51 per cent Indian students express a high need for advanced computer-related training. At CT, 43 per cent African and 36 per cent coloured students express a high need for advanced computer-related training as opposed to 30 per cent white students. At PT, 41 per cent African and 47 per cent coloured students express a high need for advanced computer-related training.

TABLE 5.38: Index of advanced computer-related needs – UCT

	High-need category	Moderate-need category	Low-need category	Total count
	Row %	Row %	Row %	
Year group				
Junior undergraduate	29	30	41	923
Senior undergraduate	23	36	40	351
Postgraduate	25	30	45	406
Disciplinary area				
Humanities	25	24	50	405
Social sciences	27	30	43	319
Economic and				
management sciences	25	39	36	399
Natural sciences	33	37	30	215
Engineering and design	—	—	—	—
Medical and health sciences	25	29	46	340
Academic performance				
<50%	34	30	36	83
50–59%	27	34	39	318
60–69%	29	29	42	737
70%+	21	35	45	465
Race				
African	36	23	41	380
White	18	35	46	897
Coloured	36	31	33	222
Indian	44	25	31	114
Gender				
Female	28	29	43	905
Male	25	34	41	769
Language				
Afrikaans	32	27	41	71
English	23	34	43	1 141
African languages	36	23	40	354
Other languages	26	32	42	95
Age in years				
Under 22	27	31	42	1 139
22–29	25	31	44	493
30 or older	33	33	33	45

The gender breakdown indicates that at UCT (28:25%), US (23:22%) and CT (38:31%) more females than males express a high need for advanced computer-related training. At UWC (43:47%) and PT (40:50%) more males than females express a high need for advanced computer-related training.

The age breakdown of the sample reveals interesting differences between the university and technikon sector. At the three universities, the results reveal that a greater proportion of younger students expresses a high need for advanced computer-related

TABLE 5.39: Index of advanced computer-related needs – US

	High-need category	Moderate-need category	Low-need category	Total count
	Row %	Row %	Row %	
Year group				
Junior undergraduate	22	36	41	911
Senior undergraduate	24	31	44	181
Postgraduate	20	35	45	183
Disciplinary area				
Humanities	28	31	41	199
Social sciences	19	32	49	330
Economic and				
management sciences	25	37	38	454
Natural sciences	19	40	41	184
Engineering and design	—	—	—	—
Medical and health sciences	15	40	45	110
Academic performance				
<50%	25	37	38	89
50–59%	22	38	41	360
60–69%	23	31	46	497
70%+	21	39	39	295
Race				
African	27	36	36	22
White	20	36	43	1 066
Coloured	33	30	38	160
Indian	13	38	50	8
Gender				
Female	23	33	44	784
Male	22	39	39	491
Language				
Afrikaans	20	37	43	834
English	26	33	42	385
African languages	20	45	35	20
Other languages	29	24	47	17
Age in years				
Under 22	22	36	41	1 054
22–29	21	34	45	191
30 or older	20	20	60	30

training. Thus, students aged 30 years and older express less high need for such training compared to students below 22 years of age. At the two technikons, a greater proportion of older students express high need for advanced computer-related training compared to younger students.

The index of advanced computer-related information needs, similar to the other indexes in this sub-section, signals that a high level of need exists across the entire region, especially among students at the HDIs. An interesting observation is that these

TABLE 5.40: Index of advanced computer-related needs – UWC

	High-need category	Moderate-need category	Low-need category	Total count
	Row %	Row %	Row %	
Year group				
Junior undergraduate	34	23	42	511
Senior undergraduate	48	24	28	469
Postgraduate	51	22	26	209
Disciplinary area				
Humanities	41	25	35	295
Social sciences	38	22	40	348
Economic and management sciences	50	25	26	295
Natural sciences	38	26	36	155
Engineering and design	—	—	—	—
Medical and health sciences	57	12	31	49
Academic performance				
<50%	36	19	45	86
50–59%	40	25	35	503
60–69%	44	27	29	398
70%+	51	21	28	136
Race				
African	38	21	41	602
White	38	38	25	8
Coloured	46	27	27	435
Indian	51	27	22	92
Gender				
Female	43	22	35	667
Male	47	26	27	327
Language				
Afrikaans	48	27	25	235
English	47	26	27	327
African languages	38	21	41	597
Other languages	75	—	25	4
Age in years				
Under 22	44	24	32	563
22–29	43	22	35	534
30 or older	35	27	38	86

indexes relate to students' awareness of their information needs, whether basic or advanced, and while some students might lack the skills required, they are not necessarily conscious of this.

Index of independent learning

The final section of the questionnaire included a number of items that aimed at measuring different modalities of independent learning. This section was designed to measure the extent to which

TABLE 5.41: Index of advanced computer-related needs – CT

	High-need category	Moderate-need category	Low-need category	Total count
	Row %	Row %	Row %	
Year group				
Junior undergraduate	36	34	30	402
Senior undergraduate	33	33	34	119
Postgraduate	27	39	34	92
Disciplinary area				
Humanities	—	—	—	—
Social sciences	47	27	26	62
Economic and management sciences	35	36	28	155
Natural sciences	—	—	—	—
Engineering and design	34	35	32	310
Medical and health sciences	15	29	56	34
Academic performance				
<50%	31	23	46	48
50–59%	33	31	36	163
60–69%	38	35	27	231
70%+	30	41	29	154
Race				
African	43	22	35	112
White	30	39	31	361
Coloured	36	33	31	120
Indian	17	50	33	6
Gender				
Female	38	34	28	232
Male	31	35	34	379
Language				
Afrikaans	26	35	38	231
English	38	37	26	261
African languages	43	25	32	107
Other languages	18	45	36	11
Age in years				
Under 22	33	35	32	419
22–29	39	31	29	147
30 or older	26	40	34	47

independent learning is being encouraged and promoted at the five institutions. Again, the first stage was to establish the factorial structure of the eleven items. A principal components analysis revealed an optimal solution of three factors explaining 53 per cent of the variance.

Factor 1 (items 5.2, 5.3, 5.4 and 5.8) may best be interpreted as relating to interactive or participative forms of learning. This factor could be interpreted as relating to learning activities in which there was some form of engagement by the learner with

TABLE 5.42: Index of advanced computer-related needs – PT

	High-need category	Moderate-need category	Low-need category	Total count
	Row %	Row %	Row %	
Year group				
Junior undergraduate	48	25	28	287
Senior undergraduate	45	25	30	216
Postgraduate	38	18	44	73
Disciplinary area				
Humanities	—	—	—	—
Social sciences	31	25	43	175
Economic and management sciences	47	24	30	88
Natural sciences	—	—	—	—
Engineering and design	55	24	21	274
Medical and health sciences	45	22	33	136
Academic performance				
<50%	31	28	41	58
50–59%	46	25	29	224
60–69%	44	24	32	224
70%+	52	22	26	95
Race				
African	41	21	38	315
White	38	13	50	8
Coloured	47	29	23	289
Indian	—	—	100	1
Gender				
Female	40	22	38	301
Male	50	26	24	371
Language				
Afrikaans	45	29	26	221
English	54	25	21	125
African languages	43	20	36	319
Other languages	50	—	50	4
Age in years				
Under 22	48	24	28	380
22–29	43	24	34	268
30 or older	33	33	33	24

other people. It is also a factor that involves learners in searching and sourcing information in a practical way and outside the classroom/lecture hall. This factor is referred to as "interactive learning".

Factor 2 (items 5.1, 5.6 and 5.7) can be interpreted as independent learning that learners engage with on their own. The primary defining feature of this factor is that it is learning which depends on a learner's personal volition. By contrast to factor 1, it does not involve engagement with others, and activities outside the environment of the lecture hall and readings. This factor is referred to as "individual learning". It could be considered to conform to a fairly conventional notion of independent learning.

The third factor (items 5.9 and 5.10) clearly refers to learning through different technologies – principally media technology. This factor is thus interpreted as independent learning which relies on other technologies as sources of information for learning. It is referred to as "media-based learning".

Following the procedure established thus far, three indices for "interactive learning", "individual learning" and "media-based learning" were created. The basic frequency distributions for each of the indices are given in charts 5.8, 5.9 and 5.10.

CHART 5.8: Frequency count of the index of interactive learning

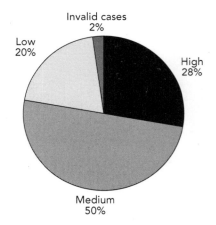

CHART 5.9: Frequency count of the index of individual learning

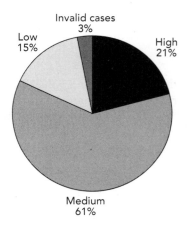

CHART 5.10: Frequency count of the index of media-based learning

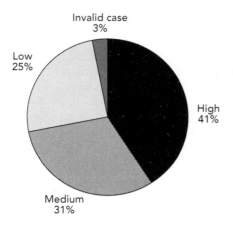

Index of interactive learning across the region by institution

The following table suggests differences between universities and technikons, with a greater proportion of students at the technikons than the universities reporting high levels of interactive learning (CT 43% and PT 33% of the proportion of students). The technikons also report far fewer cases in the lower categories of this index (CT 8% and PT 11% of the proportion of students) as opposed to the universities (UCT 27%; US 22%; UWC 21%).

GRAPH 5.8: Institutional results for the index of interactive learning

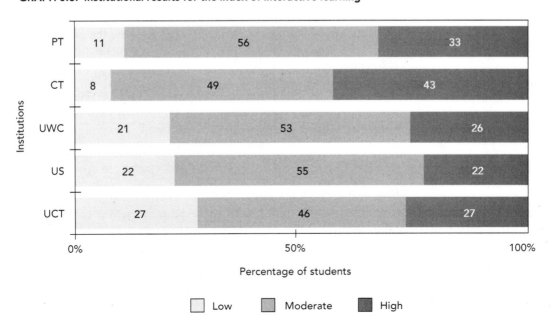

Index of interactive learning of the total sample by key variables

Table 5.43 below indicates interactive learning across the year levels for the total sample. Thus, postgraduate students (39%) engage more often in activities such as fieldwork and practical assignments compared to first-year students (25%).

With respect to disciplinary domains, students engaged in forms of interactive learning are more likely to be found in medical and health sciences (45%), engineering and design (35%), and social sciences (35%), than in the natural sciences (24%), economic and management sciences (20%) and humanities (17%). The high incidence of this factor in the social sciences is most likely due to the fact that education students were included in this domain. These results are not too surprising as they reflect the fact that it is the more applied and natural sciences in which students are more likely to engage in activities that constitute interactive learning.

Of significance is the relationship between interactive learning and academic performance. The results indicate that students who report high performance scores also, are more likely to engage in independent interactive learning. Thus, for example, 32 per cent of students who report scores of 70 per cent and above are in the high interactive learning category compared to 21 per cent of students with scores of less than 50 per cent. This suggests that better performing students are also more interactive learners.

The racial breakdown reveals an interesting picture. The results suggest that it is coloured students (31%) followed by African students (28%), then Indian students (26%) and finally white students (26%) who indicate that they are more often engaged in forms of interactive learning. However, it should be noted that the difference in percentage terms is not large between the groups.

Gender analysis reveals that a greater proportion of females (30%) compared to males (26%) are likely to engage in forms of interactive learning often.

"Of significance is the relationship between interactive learning and academic performance."

The table indicates that there is a strong relationship between age and students who report high interactive learning. Thus, students in the age range 22 to 29 (32%) and 30 and above (30%) are more likely to engage in forms of interactive learning than those aged younger than 22 (26%).

Index of interactive learning by institution and variable

The tables below (tables 5.44 to 5.48) indicate that at UCT, US, UWC and CT forms of interactive learning in the category "high" increases across the respective year levels. The one slight difference is that the proportion of students for the "high" category at UCT declines from 26 per cent in the first year to 24 per cent in the third year, but increases to 32 per cent in the postgraduate cohort. The most marked shifts in this respect are at UWC where

TABLE 5.43: Index of interactive learning – Total sample

	High interactive learning	Medium interactive learning	Low interactive learning	Total count
	Row %	Row %	Row %	
Year group				
Junior undergraduate	25	54	21	3 157
Senior undergraduate	29	49	22	1 334
Postgraduate	39	46	15	971
Disciplinary area				
Humanities	17	53	30	905
Social sciences	35	49	16	1 248
Economic and management sciences	20	49	31	1 432
Natural sciences	24	64	12	559
Engineering and design	35	55	10	584
Medical and health sciences	45	46	9	678
Academic performance				
<50%	21	58	21	365
50–59%	26	53	21	1 583
60–69%	29	51	20	2 095
70%+	32	48	20	1 147
Race				
African	28	55	16	1 449
White	26	51	23	2 344
Coloured	31	49	20	1 233
Indian	27	47	27	221
Gender				
Female	30	51	19	2 913
Male	26	52	22	2 531
Language				
Afrikaans	28	52	20	1 594
English	29	48	23	2 247
African languages	29	55	16	1 415
Other languages	20	48	32	132
Age in years				
Under 22	26	52	21	3 576
22–29	32	49	19	1 639
30 or older	32	53	16	234

it increases from 19 per cent of the proportion of the sample in the first year to 45 per cent in the postgraduate, and at CT where the first-year proportion of students is 39 per cent increasing to 54 per cent in the postgraduate year.

Analysis by disciplinary domain suggests marked variation across the five institutions in respect of the high interactive learning category. AT UCT and US, the disciplinary domain which has the largest proportion of students for the high category is medical and health sciences (UCT 54%, US 37%) compared to social sciences at UWC (42%). At CT, the disciplinary domain which has the highest proportion of students for the high category is economic and management sciences (69%), whereas at PT it is the medical and health sciences (41%).

The relationship between academic performance and high interactive learning is evident in the institutional profiles but not as clear-cut as the total sample table above reveals. At UCT, US, UWC and PT, it is evident that a greater proportion of postgraduate students are engaged in forms of interactive learning than first-years. However, there is no obvious pattern between students who report scores of 50 to 59 per cent and 60 to 69 per cent and high independent interactive learning for UWC and PT. CT results are interesting as they indicate an almost even number of students in the high interactive-learning category and performance scores. The proportion of students for CT are 42 per cent for the score below 50 per cent, 44 per cent for the score 50 to 59 per cent, 42 per cent for the score 60 to 69 per cent and 70 per cent.

The racial breakdown for UCT and US indicates that black students in general report being more involved in forms of inter-active learning than white students. However, the differences are not large in percentage terms. At CT, there is a fairly even racial breakdown across the different racial groups in respect of high interactive learning. At UWC and PT in respect of black students, the results indicate that there is a greater proportion of coloured students than African students in the high category.

At four of the five institutions, a greater proportion of females than males report being engaged in high interactive learning. It is only at PT where the results reveal more males in the high category than females.

Unlike the total results for the entire sample, there is no obvious pattern between age and the high interactive-learning category at the five institutions. At UCT, there is a decline from 27 per cent in the category below 22 to 24 per cent in the age range 30 and above, while the percentage of students for the 22 to 29 group is 28 per cent. At US, there is an increase from 20 per cent for the under-22s to 38 per cent in the 22 to 29 range, but a decline to 33 per cent in the 30 and above cohort. At UWC, the pattern is the same as at US, though the figures are different. At CT, interestingly there is a consistent increase across the year indicating a strong relationship between age and the high interactive-learning category. At PT there is an increase from the under-22s (33%) to age 30 and above (39%).

There are two important features of the institutional profiles for the index of interactive learning. First, the results indicate some differences between the universities and technikons in respect of the learning activities associated with interactive learning. It is evident that a greater proportion of students at the technikons report high forms of interactive learning than those at the universities. Secondly, it is important to note that high proportions of the sample at all five institutions fall in the high/moderate

TABLE 5.44: Index of interactive learning – UCT

	High interactive learning	Medium interactive learning	Low interactive learning	Total count
	Row %	Row %	Row %	
Year group				
Junior undergraduate	26	45	29	941
Senior undergraduate	24	45	31	350
Postgraduate	32	50	18	410
Disciplinary area				
Humanities	13	44	43	407
Social sciences	31	48	21	325
Economic and management sciences	18	40	42	400
Natural sciences	21	70	9	220
Engineering and design	—	—	—	—
Medical and health sciences	54	40	6	347
Academic performance				
<50%	21	61	18	85
50–59%	22	48	30	326
60–69%	27	46	28	743
70%+	31	44	24	469
Race				
African	27	50	23	395
White	26	45	29	902
Coloured	27	46	26	223
Indian	31	40	29	115
Gender				
Female	30	46	24	923
Male	24	47	29	772
Language				
Afrikaans	32	50	18	72
English	28	44	28	1 145
African languages	27	52	21	368
Other languages	15	49	35	97
Age in years				
Under 22	27	45	28	1 157
22–29	28	48	23	495
30 or older	24	50	26	46

category of the index. This suggests that forms of interactive learning are possibly occurring at higher-education institutions in the region.

Index of individual learning across institutions in the region

The results reported in the table reflect a clustering among UCT, UWC and PT on the one hand, and US and CT on the other. A higher proportion of students at the former institutions report levels of individual learning (UCT 26%, UWC 24% and PT 23%

TABLE 5.45: Index of interactive learning – US

	High interactive learning	Medium interactive learning	Low interactive learning	Total count
	Row %	Row %	Row %	
Year group				
Junior undergraduate	18	60	23	912
Senior undergraduate	30	46	25	179
Postgraduate	42	43	15	183
Disciplinary area				
Humanities	38	32	31	199
Social sciences	36	47	17	330
Economic and management sciences	10	56	34	453
Natural sciences	21	66	14	184
Engineering and design	—	—	—	—
Medical and health sciences	37	47	15	110
Academic performance				
<50%	21	53	26	89
50–59%	20	58	23	360
60–69%	24	55	21	497
70%+	25	54	21	294
Race				
African	23	64	14	22
White	21	56	23	1 064
Coloured	32	51	18	160
Indian	25	50	25	8
Gender				
Female	25	56	19	783
Male	19	55	26	491
Language				
Afrikaans	24	53	24	831
English	20	61	19	387
African languages	50	35	15	20
Other languages	29	65	6	17
Age in years				
Under 22	20	59	21	1 056
22–29	38	38	24	188
30 or older	33	47	20	30

respectively), while only ten per cent of the proportion of students report being inactive in this area. This contrasts with reports of activity at US and CT where only 15 and 17 per cent of the proportion of students respectively report high individual learning activity, while a wider gap appears in the area of low activity with 31 and 16 per cent of the proportion of students respectively reporting minimal activity.

Overall, less than a third of the student sample is engaged in forms of individual learning, such as essay writing, on a regular

TABLE 5.46: Index of interactive learning – UWC

	High interactive learning	Medium interactive learning	Low interactive learning	Total count
	Row %	Row %	Row %	
Year group				
Junior undergraduate	19	58	22	513
Senior undergraduate	26	52	22	470
Postgraduate	45	41	14	212
Disciplinary area				
Humanities	18	59	23	299
Social sciences	42	47	11	354
Economic and management sciences	14	53	33	335
Natural sciences	32	53	15	155
Engineering and design	—	—	—	—
Medical and health sciences	31	57	12	51
Academic performance				
<50%	15	56	28	85
50–59%	20	56	24	509
60–69%	34	51	15	399
70%+	32	47	21	135
Race				
African	26	57	17	607
White	38	63	—	8
Coloured	28	47	25	437
Indian	22	52	26	91
Gender				
Female	30	51	20	672
Male	21	56	22	517
Language				
Afrikaans	30	48	22	237
English	25	48	27	326
African languages	26	57	17	602
Other languages	25	—	75	4
Age in years				
Under 22	24	54	22	561
22–29	29	50	20	540
30 or older	23	61	16	88

basis. The average proportion of students recording low levels of individual learning across the whole sample is a very low 21 per cent. Most students report moderate levels of individual learning, on average 63 per cent of the proportion of students in the sample. This suggests that this form of activity is not by any means absent from current learning practice.

TABLE 5.47: Index of interactive learning – CT

	High interactive learning	Medium interactive learning	Low interactive learning	Total count
	Row %	Row %	Row %	
Year group				
Junior undergraduate	39	53	7	404
Senior undergraduate	45	43	13	119
Postgraduate	54	37	9	92
Disciplinary area				
Humanities	—	—	—	—
Social sciences	47	52	2	62
Economic and				
management sciences	69	30	1	155
Natural sciences	—	—	—	—
Engineering and design	32	56	13	311
Medical and health sciences	17	63	20	35
Academic performance				
<50%	42	44	15	48
50–59%	44	49	7	164
60–69%	42	50	7	232
70%+	42	47	11	154
Race				
African	45	47	8	112
White	42	49	8	352
Coloured	41	50	9	121
Indian	17	83	—	6
Gender				
Female	48	44	7	232
Male	39	51	9	381
Language				
Afrikaans	36	55	9	231
English	46	46	8	263
African languages	47	46	7	107
Other languages	27	45	27	11
Age in years				
Under 22	40	51	9	421
22–29	48	43	9	147
30 or older	51	45	4	47

Index of individual learning of the total sample

Table 5.49 below indicates that individual learning for the high (often) category increases across all the year levels for the total sample. Thus, postgraduate students (32%) are more likely than third-year students (24%) who are more likely than first-year students (17%) to engage in forms of independent learning. It is important to note that the proportion of students almost doubles from the first to the postgraduate years.

TABLE 5.48: Index of interactive learning – PT

	High interactive learning	Medium interactive learning	Low interactive learning	Total count
	Row %	Row %	Row %	
Year group				
Junior undergraduate	31	58	11	387
Senior undergraduate	36	54	10	216
Postgraduate	30	55	15	74
Disciplinary area				
Humanities	—	—	—	—
Social sciences	24	59	18	177
Economic and management sciences	13	71	16	89
Natural sciences	—	—	—	—
Engineering and design	39	54	7	273
Medical and health sciences	41	50	8	135
Academic performance				
<50%	12	78	10	58
50–59%	39	49	12	224
60–69%	29	59	12	224
70%+	39	57	4	95
Race				
African	29	61	10	313
White	38	63	—	8
Coloured	35	52	12	292
Indian	—	100	—	1
Gender				
Female	30	58	12	303
Male	34	55	11	370
Language				
Afrikaans	33	54	13	223
English	40	49	11	126
African languages	29	61	10	318
Other languages	67	—	33	3
Age in years				
Under 22	33	54	13	381
22–29	31	60	9	269
30 or older	39	48	13	23

The disciplinary-domain results reveal that a greater proportion of social sciences (34%) and humanities (34%) students engage often in forms of individual learning than other disciplines. In certain cases the proportion of students for these disciplines are almost twice or thrice than that of the others. This is not surprising as the questions that made up this index emphasise writing essays and verbal classroom engagement, practices that are not necessarily prevalent in the other disciplines.

Graph 5.9: Institutional results of the index of individual learning

PT	10	67	23
CT	16	67	17
UWC	10	65	25
US	31	54	15
UCT	10	64	26

0%   50%   100%

Percentage of students

☐ Low   ◻ Moderate   ■ High

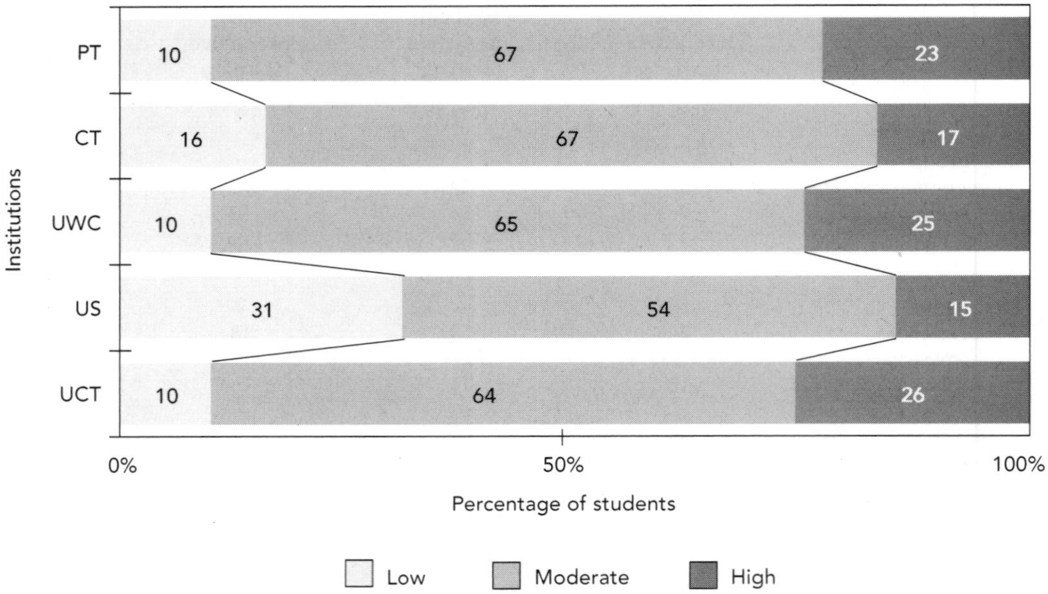

Table 5.49 suggests a strong relationship between reported academic performance and the high individual-learning category with marked differences between reported scores of less than 50 per cent and 28 per cent, and that of 70 per cent or more. It is important to note that the proportion of students almost doubles between scores of below 50 per cent and that of 70 per cent. This strongly suggests that high performers are those students who engage in individual learning.

The racial breakdown indicates that a greater proportion of African (24%) and coloured (21%) students are likely to engage in individual learning than white (20%) and Indian students (18%). Note that the difference is not high for all the racial groups.

There are no important gender differences in respect of individual learning activities. The age profile reveals that older, mature students are more likely to engage in forms of individual learning than the younger cohort of the total sample. Thus, 37 per cent of the proportion of students aged 30 and older are in the high individual-learning category compared to 18 per cent of the proportion of students aged below 22, more than twice the number.

Index of individual learning by institutions and key variables

The institutional tables confirm the pattern of high individual learning revealed for the total sample for year level. In general, at all institutions there is an increase in the proportion of postgraduate students in the "high" category compared to the proportion of

TABLE 5.49: Index of individual learning – Total sample

	High interactive learning	Medium interactive learning	Low interactive learning	Total count
	Row %	Row %	Row %	
Year group				
Junior undergraduate	17	63	20	3 156
Senior undergraduate	24	66	11	1 335
Postgraduate	32	58	10	971
Disciplinary area				
Humanities	34	63	3	905
Social sciences	34	60	6	559
Economic and management sciences	14	71	16	584
Natural sciences	9	58	34	559
Engineering and design	14	71	16	584
Medical and health sciences	15	68	17	679
Academic performance				
<50%	12	64	25	365
50–59%	16	67	17	1 583
60–69%	23	63	14	2 094
70%+	28	58	14	1 147
Race				
African	24	68	8	1 449
White	20	59	21	2 345
Coloured	21	63	16	1 233
Indian	18	70	12	221
Gender				
Female	22	61	17	2 914
Male	21	64	15	2 530
Language				
Afrikaans	17	58	25	1 594
English	22	63	14	2 247
African languages	25	67	8	1 414
Other languages	27	63	10	133
Age in years				
Under 22	18	63	19	3 574
22–29	27	63	10	1 640
30 or older	37	60	3	235

students in the first year. Furthermore, for three of the five institutions (UCT, UWC and PT) there is an increase across all year levels. At US and CT the proportion of students drops between the first and third year. The most important result is at PT where 41 per cent of postgraduate students report in the "high" individual-learning category compared to 20 per cent of its first-year sample.

At the three universities it is not surprising to find a prevalence of "high" individual learning in the disciplines of humanities and social sciences. What is important to note is the low proportion of students for "high" individual learning at the three universities. At UCT the proportion of students in the high category for the disciplinary domain of natural sciences is six per cent, at US it is two per cent but at UWC 20 per cent. At the two technikons, the disciplinary domains of humanities and social sciences are the ones where a greater proportion of students engage in forms of individual learning. The proportion of students in the natural sciences at the technikons is low for forms of individual learning but not as marked as at the universities. This result is possibly explained, as mentioned previously, by the fact that the kinds of learning associated with this index in the questionnaire are most likely to be found in the humanities and social sciences disciplines.

The results for academic performance indicate that there is a strong relationship between performance and the high individual-learning category. Without exception, the results for the institutions indicate there is a greater proportion of students who report scores of 70 per cent or more, compared to those who indicate scores of below 50 per cent. This is most marked at UCT where 37 per cent of the proportion of students in the high individual-learning category report scores of 70 per cent and more, whereas only 13 per cent of the proportion of students report a score of below 50 per cent.

Breakdown of the sample by race for each institution indicates that at UCT a greater proportion of white students (28%) are in the "high" category, at US it is African students (32%) and also at CT (22%). At UWC and PT the results indicate that a greater proportion of African and coloured students are in the "high" category. The tables indicate that in most instances the greatest proportion of students in the high category are African.

The gender breakdown reveals that a greater proportion of females than males at UCT (female 27%, male 25%) , US (female 16%, male 13%) and CT (female 21%, male 15%) report high individual learning. It is the reverse at UWC (male 25%, female 23%) and PT (male 24%, female 22%) where a greater proportion of males than females report high individual learning.

Without exception, at all institutions there is a strong relationship between age and high individual learning. The direction of the relationship is in favour of increasing age. Thus, the proportion of students aged 30 and older in the high category for the index is substantially higher at all institutions as opposed to the proportion of students in the age range below 22 years. This is perhaps more marked at UCT and US where 40 per cent of their proportion of students in the high category are aged 30 and older.

A notable feature of the results for this index is, similar to the index of interactive learning, the relationship between the variables of race, performance and age concerning forms of individual learning. For example, high performers are also those students who are more likely to engage more often in forms of individual learning.

TABLE 5.50: Index of individual learning – UCT

	High individual learning	Medium individual learning	Low individual learning	Total count
	Row %	Row %	Row %	
Year group				
Junior undergraduate	20	67	13	940
Senior undergraduate	29	65	7	350
Postgraduate	36	56	8	410
Disciplinary area				
Humanities	41	57	2	407
Social sciences	39	59	1	325
Economic and management sciences	18	69	13	400
Natural sciences	6	65	29	220
Engineering and design	—	—	—	—
Medical and health sciences	16	69	15	346
Academic performance				
<50%	13	65	22	85
50–59%	16	71	13	326
60–69%	24	66	10	742
70%+	37	56	7	469
Race				
African	23	66	11	394
White	28	62	10	902
Coloured	24	63	13	223
Indian	18	73	9	115
Gender				
Female	27	62	11	922
Male	25	65	10	772
Language				
Afrikaans	38	58	4	72
English	26	63	11	1 145
African languages	24	66	10	367
Other languages	27	64	9	97
Age in years				
Under 22	22	65	12	1 156
22–29	31	62	7	495
30 or older	46	52	2	46

Index of media-based learning across institutions in the region

Table 5.55 (see p.163) echoes the frequently encountered differences between HDIs and HAIs. Once again, a greater proportion of UWC (47%) and PT (49%) students report high levels of media-based learning (learning from other information sources such as newspapers and radio) compared to the three HAIs. The pattern holds for "low" reports of media-based learning with a

TABLE 5.51: Index of individual learning – US

	High individual learning	Medium individual learning	Low individual learning	Total count
	Row %	Row %	Row %	
Year group				
Junior undergraduate	12	52	36	912
Senior undergraduate	23	65	12	179
Postgraduate	22	55	22	184
Disciplinary area				
Humanities	33	62	5	199
Social sciences	26	59	15	330
Economic and management sciences	6	48	46	453
Natural sciences	2	49	48	184
Engineering and design	—	—	—	—
Medical and health sciences	6	61	32	111
Academic performance				
<50%	9	53	38	89
50–59%	11	56	32	360
60–69%	18	54	27	498
70%+	15	54	31	294
Race				
African	32	68	—	22
White	15	57	28	1 065
Coloured	19	55	26	160
Indian	—	63	38	8
Gender				
Female	16	53	30	784
Male	13	56	31	491
Language				
Afrikaans	14	51	35	832
English	17	59	24	387
African languages	30	60	10	20
Other languages	29	59	12	17
Age in years				
Under 22	14	53	33	1 056
22–29	19	59	22	189
30 or older	43	53	3	30

smaller proportion of students at the HDIs in this category (UWC 18%, PT 16%) suggesting that more media-based learning occurs at these institutions. The average for the HAIs shows that as many as 30 per cent of the students in their sample report low levels of media-based learning. This suggests that, while the HDIs are better disposed towards independent learning, the HAIs require greater encouragement in this direction.

TABLE 5.52: Index of individual learning – UWC

	High individual learning	Medium individual learning	Low individual learning	Total count
	Row %	Row %	Row %	
Year group				
Junior undergraduate	22	70	9	513
Senior undergraduate	23	62	15	470
Postgraduate	30	64	6	211
Disciplinary area				
Humanities	33	62	5	199
Social sciences	26	59	15	330
Economic and management sciences	6	48	46	453
Natural sciences	2	49	48	184
Engineering and design	—	—	—	—
Medical and health sciences	6	61	32	111
Academic performance				
<50%	15	69	15	85
50–59%	18	69	13	508
60–69%	30	63	7	399
70%+	33	57	10	135
Race				
African	24	69	7	607
White	50	25	25	8
Coloured	22	64	14	436
Indian	21	66	13	91
Gender				
Female	23	66	11	672
Male	25	65	10	516
Language				
Afrikaans	22	67	11	236
English	23	61	16	326
African languages	25	68	7	602
Other languages	25	50	25	4
Age in years				
Under 22	20	68	12	561
22–29	26	63	11	539
30 or older	34	64	2	88

Index of media-based learning of the total sample

Table 5.55 (see p.163) below indicates that there is an increase in media-based activities across the year levels for the total sample. Thus, a greater proportion of postgraduate students are likely to obtain and use information from principally media-based sources than first-year students.

The table also reveals that at least a third of the sample, and in most cases more than this, in all disciplines engage in media-based

TABLE 5.53: Index of individual learning – CT

	High individual learning	Medium individual learning	Low individual learning	Total count
	Row %	Row %	Row %	
Year group				
Junior undergraduate	16	66	18	404
Senior undergraduate	14	75	11	120
Postgraduate	29	60	11	92
Disciplinary area				
Humanities	—	—	—	—
Social sciences	35	58	6	62
Economic and management sciences	21	65	14	155
Natural sciences	—	—	—	—
Engineering and design	11	71	18	312
Medical and health sciences	3	66	31	35
Academic performance				
<50%	10	63	27	48
50–59%	18	65	18	164
60–69%	16	72	12	232
70%+	22	65	13	154
Race				
African	22	68	10	112
White	18	68	14	362
Coloured	13	61	25	122
Indian	—	83	17	6
Gender				
Female	21	65	14	233
Male	15	68	17	381
Language				
Afrikaans	16	63	22	232
English	17	70	13	263
African languages	24	66	9	107
Other languages	9	82	9	11
Age in years				
Under 22	13	69	18	421
22–29	26	61	13	148
30 or older	34	64	2	47

learning activities. This is particularly prevalent in the disciplines of economic and management sciences (46%), social sciences (45%) and humanities (44%).

The results by academic-performance scores are fairly even, averaging at about 40 per cent of the proportion of students in the high category. The exception to this trend is the score of 50 to 59 per cent where 44 per cent of the total sample fall in the high media-based-learning category.

TABLE 5.54: Index of individual learning – PT

	High individual learning	Medium individual learning	Low individual learning	Total count
	Row %	Row %	Row %	
Year group				
Junior undergraduate	20	67	13	387
Senior undergraduate	22	70	7	216
Postgraduate	41	55	4	74
Disciplinary area				
Humanities	—	—	—	—
Social sciences	40	54	7	177
Economic and management sciences	17	74	9	89
Natural sciences	—	—	—	—
Engineering and design	17	71	13	272
Medical and health sciences	18	72	10	136
Academic performance				
<50%	10	71	19	58
50–59%	20	74	6	225
60–69%	28	58	13	223
70%+	27	66	6	95
Race				
African	25	68	8	314
White	38	50	13	8
Coloured	22	66	12	292
Indian	—	100	—	1
Gender				
Female	22	66	12	303
Male	24	68	8	370
Language				
Afrikaans	19	67	14	222
English	22	67	10	126
African languages	25	68	8	318
Other languages	75	25	—	4
Age in years				
Under 22	19	68	13	380
22–29	27	66	7	269
30 or older	29	67	4	24

Table 5.55 indicates that a greater proportion of black students in general and African students in particular (48%) feature in the "high" category than of white students (37%).

The gender breakdown for the sample suggests that a greater proportion of males (45%) than females (39%) are likely to engage in media-based learning.

Consistent with the other two indexes of independent learning, the table reveals that the proportion of students in the high

GRAPH 5.10: Index of media-based learning

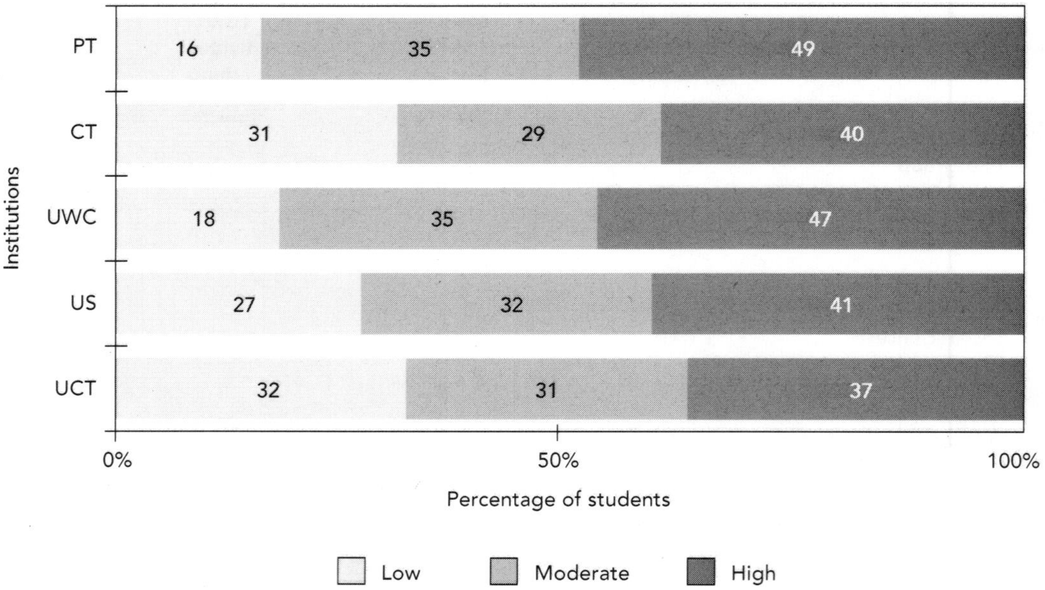

category increases with age. Thus, a greater proportion of students aged 30 and more (51%) compared to those aged below 22 (39%) are likely to engage in media-based learning activities.

Index of media-based learning by institutions and key variables

The index of media-based learning suggests that a large number of students obtain information from other sources. The tables also indicate that this is strongly related to year level. Thus, a greater proportion of postgraduate students (4th year) are more likely to obtain information from other sources than the first-year cohort. However, the data does not indicate precisely what information is obtained. Nonetheless, it suggests that other information sources play an important role in the learning experiences of students. The most significant results are at UWC and PT where the proportion of postgraduate students, who are in the high media-based-learning category, are 58 and 57 per cent respectively.

At the three universities and PT, the disciplinary domains, where students rely on other sources of information, are the humanities and social sciences followed quite closely by economic and management sciences. At CT, the most important disciplinary domain is economic and management sciences. A pattern that emerges is that it is mainly the humanities and social sciences disciplinary domains where there is a prevalence of students in the "high" media-based category.

The interesting pattern is that there is no uniform increase across all performance scores for media-based learning at all three

TABLE 5.55: Index of media-based learning – Total sample

	High media-based learning	Medium media-based learning	Low media-based learning	Total count
	Row %	Row %	Row %	
Year group				
Junior undergraduate	40	34	26	3 137
Senior undergraduate	43	32	26	1 329
Postgraduate	46	29	25	968
Disciplinary area				
Humanities	44	32	24	897
Social sciences	45	33	22	1 240
Economic and management sciences	46	34	19	1 425
Natural sciences	30	28	43	558
Engineering and design	36	31	33	582
Medical and health sciences	38	33	29	676
Academic performance				
<50%	39	34	27	363
50–59%	44	33	23	1 576
60–69%	40	32	28	2 083
70%+	41	32	27	1 145
Race				
African	48	33	19	1 431
White	37	31	32	1 228
Coloured	44	34	22	1 232
Indian	41	30	29	218
Gender				
Female	39	34	27	2 897
Male	45	30	25	2 519
Language				
Afrikaans	41	33	26	1 594
English	39	32	29	2 236
African languages	48	33	18	1 398
Other languages	31	26	43	133
Age in years				
Under 22	39	33	28	3 557
22–29	46	32	22	1 632
30 or older	51	31	19	232

universities. For example, at UCT, a greater proportion of students who report scores 50 to 59 per cent (41%) are found in the high-need category than those with results of 60 to 69 per cent (34%). UWC is the only university where there is a relationship between performance scores and media-based learning activities. The interesting result is for CT, where there is marked inverse relationship between performance scores and the proportion of students in the high category. Thus, the table indicates 63 per cent of the proportion of students at the institution are in the high

TABLE 5.56: Index of media-based learning – UCT

	High media-based learning	Medium media-based learning	Low media-based learning	Total count
	Row %	Row %	Row %	
Year group				
Junior undergraduate	35	31	35	931
Senior undergraduate	38	31	31	350
Postgraduate	41	30	29	406
Disciplinary area				
Humanities	39	32	29	402
Social sciences	37	31	31	321
Economic and management sciences	40	31	29	399
Natural sciences	30	27	43	220
Engineering and design	—	—	—	—
Medical and health sciences	35	31	34	343
Academic performance				
<50%	32	29	39	84
50–59%	41	30	30	321
60–69%	34	32	34	740
70%+	40	29	31	468
Race				
African	42	31	27	384
White	35	30	36	901
Coloured	35	37	28	222
Indian	43	23	34	114
Gender				
Female	34	31	35	914
Male	40	30	30	767
Language				
Afrikaans	36	36	28	72
English	36	31	33	1 143
African languages	41	31	28	357
Other languages	29	24	47	97
Age in years				
Under 22	34	31	35	1 149
22–29	42	30	28	490
30 or older	58	18	24	45

category for reported performance scores of below 50 per cent, but only 37 per cent of the proportion of students who report a result of 70 per cent or more.

The racial breakdown indicates that for UCT, US and CT, a greater proportion of black students in general utilise and obtain other sources of information. At UWC and PT, a greater proportion of African than coloured students engage in media-based learning, but this is only marginally so in the case of PT.

In the case of gender, a greater proportion of males than

TABLE 5.57: Index of media-based learning – US

	High media-based learning	Medium media-based learning	Low media-based learning	Total count
	Row %	Row %	Row %	
Year group				
Junior undergraduate	41	34	25	909
Senior undergraduate	37	30	33	178
Postgraduate	41	27	32	184
Disciplinary area				
Humanities	38	32	31	196
Social sciences	44	31	25	330
Economic and management sciences	48	37	15	452
Natural sciences	23	25	52	184
Engineering and design	—	—	—	—
Medical and health sciences	35	28	37	111
Academic performance				
<50%	34	39	27	88
50–59%	40	34	26	360
60–69%	43	30	27	495
70%+	40	32	28	294
Race				
African	59	23	18	22
White	39	33	28	1 061
Coloured	49	31	20	160
Indian	50	25	25	8
Gender				
Female	40	32	28	783
Male	42	32	25	488
Language				
Afrikaans	39	32	29	831
English	42	33	25	384
African languages	50	35	15	20
Other languages	47	24	29	17
Age in years				
Under 22	40	33	27	1 053
22–29	41	30	29	189
30 or older	59	21	21	29

females engage in forms of media-based learning, with CT being the exception where a greater proportion of females (41%) than males (39%) are in the high media-based-learning category.

At UCT, US, UWC and CT increasing age is strongly associated with the high media-based-learning category. Thus, it is the case that a greater proportion of students aged 30 years and more are more likely to engage in media-based learning compared to students aged below 22 years. In this respect, it is important to note that at UCT (58%), US (59%) and UWC (51%) more than

TABLE 5.58: Index of media-based learning – UWC

	High media-based learning	Medium media-based learning	Low media-based learning	Total count
	Row %	Row %	Row %	
Year group				
Junior undergraduate	42	37	20	505
Senior undergraduate	47	33	20	468
Postgraduate	58	31	11	212
Disciplinary area				
Humanities	55	32	13	299
Social sciences	48	37	15	350
Economic and management sciences	45	34	21	330
Natural sciences	36	32	32	154
Engineering and design	—	—	—	—
Medical and health sciences	45	41	14	51
Academic performance				
<50%	36	42	21	85
50–59%	47	35	18	506
60–69%	47	33	20	395
70%+	49	34	16	134
Race				
African	50	34	15	601
White	25	63	13	8
Coloured	44	34	22	436
Indian	37	38	25	89
Gender				
Female	43	37	19	665
Male	51	31	18	514
Language				
Afrikaans	40	36	24	237
English	45	34	21	320
African languages	51	34	15	598
Other languages	50	25	25	4
Age in years				
Under 22	43	35	22	555
22–29	50	34	16	637
30 or older	51	37	13	87

half of the total sample aged 30 and older were in the high media-based-learning category.

As the other indexes of independent learning indicate, this index supports the finding that students who report high performance scores are also more often able, and likely, to obtain information from other media sources. Age also seems to be related to students' engagement with media-based learning. In this respect it is evident that a greater proportion of mature students report in the "high" media-based-learning category than others. The tables

TABLE 5.59: Index of media-based learning – CT

	High media-based learning	Medium media-based learning	Low media-based learning	Total count
	Row %	Row %	Row %	
Year group				
Junior undergraduate	39	32	29	404
Senior undergraduate	39	25	36	118
Postgraduate	46	23	32	92
Disciplinary area				
Humanities	—	—	—	—
Social sciences	48	34	18	62
Economic and management sciences	59	30	11	155
Natural sciences	—	—	—	—
Engineering and design	28	28	44	310
Medical and health sciences	43	26	31	35
Academic performance				
<50%	63	23	15	48
50–59%	45	27	28	164
60–69%	35	30	35	230
70%+	37	31	32	154
Race				
African	51	31	18	111
White	35	28	37	361
Coloured	43	31	25	122
Indian	37	31	32	6
Gender				
Female	41	31	28	232
Male	39	28	33	380
Language				
Afrikaans	38	27	35	231
English	37	30	33	263
African languages	54	30	16	106
Other languages	9	45	45	11
Age in years				
Under 22	38	30	32	419
22–29	45	25	30	148
30 or older	45	35	21	47

also indicate that media-based learning is becoming an important source of information for all students. Thus, institutions need to engage with this shift in learning.

Conclusion

This chapter has highlighted and discussed students' information abilities and needs in accordance with the indexes which capture various dimensions of information literacy as discussed in

TABLE 5.60: Index of media-based learning – PT

	High media-based learning	Medium media-based learning	Low media-based learning	Total count
	Row %	Row %	Row %	
Year group				
Junior undergraduate	48	37	15	388
Senior undergraduate	47	34	19	215
Postgraduate	57	28	15	74
Disciplinary area				
Humanities	—	—	—	—
Social sciences	55	29	15	177
Economic and management sciences	49	44	7	89
Natural sciences	—	—	—	—
Engineering and design	44	34	22	272
Medical and health sciences	46	40	13	136
Academic performance				
<50%	41	33	26	58
50–59%	47	36	18	225
60–69%	50	35	14	223
70%+	46	43	11	95
Race				
African	49	35	16	313
White	63	25	13	8
Coloured	48	36	16	292
Indian	100	—	—	1
Gender				
Female	43	41	17	303
Male	53	31	16	370
Language				
Afrikaans	50	38	12	223
English	44	32	24	126
African languages	49	34	16	317
Other languages	50	50	—	4
Age in years				
Under 22	47	36	17	381
22–29	51	34	15	268
30 or older	42	38	21	24

Chapter 2. The discussion of abilities and needs has taken into account key variables of information literacy in the South African context such as race and gender.

The indexes of information literacy have generally shown that at least a third of the students in the higher-education sector express information needs and lack ability in the dimensions identified.

In terms of a cross- institutional profile, the results indicate differences between the HDIs and the HAIs showing that black students generally experience greater need for information-literacy interventions. The results further indicate some differences between the technikons and the universities. Furthermore, the results suggest that disciplinary domains influence information competencies. It is also apparent that gender, academic performance and age are important factors which have a bearing in levels of information literacy, suggesting that women, poor academic performers and younger students need concentrations of information-literacy education.

The following chapter considers the variables that explain the pattern of responses discussed above.

Notes

[1] It is important to note that the results for this index are based on the first four items of section C of the questionnaire and that they differ from the results for confidence when all nine items of the questionnaire are considered (cf. chapter 6, index of confidence).

[2] Figures for the columns "not very confident" and "not confident and inactive" have been combined to provide a read of levels of minimal confidence.

[3] Figures for white students at UWC and PT are not reported as the sample in both cases was eight. At the two institutions coloured students (UWC 22%, PT 16%) also fall in the high-need category.

6

Factors Explaining Students' Information-Literacy – Abilities and Needs

As mentioned previously, the data analysis investigated which variables explain students' responses to each item of the questionnaire using the CHAID facility of the SPSS programme. CHAID analysis enables the researcher to determine which of the variables identified in this study such as race or gender best explain the pattern of student responses regarding their information-literacy abilities and needs. This analysis generates a report with a listing of the most important predictor variables with a breakdown of the frequency counts for the items. This chapter reports on and discusses this analysis. However, it only focuses on the most important predictor variables. Thus, only the first variable output by CHAID is discussed.[1]

Index of confidence[2]

The index of confidence focuses on items 3.1 to 3.4 of the questionnaire. CHAID analysis indicates that the two most important predictor variables for this index are race and institution. In other words, differences in students' responses to the items are related to either their race or the institution where they are based.

Specifically, for items 3.1 and 3.4 race is the best predictor variable in accounting for the response of students. In other words, the extent to which students are prepared to act as group leaders or tackle an assignment is related to race. The results indicate that when students work in a group (item 3.1), white students are more likely to act as the leader (46%) followed by coloured (32%) and then African students (32%). For item 3.4, white students (48%) are the most eager to tackle challenging assignments followed by African students (45%), then Indian (43%) and finally coloured (38%) students.

The most important predictor variable for items 3.2 and 3.3 is institution. Thus, the university or technikon where students study explains whether students answer lecturers' questions in class or whether they speak in class when questions are asked. For 3.2, the results indicate that students who are eager to answer lecturers' questions in class are first from PT (33%), secondly from UWC (27%), thirdly from CT (25%) and then equally from UCT and US (17%). For item 3.3 the results indicate the following institutional order: CT and PT (38%), US and UWC (29%), UCT (26%). This indicates that students at the two technikons are more likely to speak in class than those at the universities.

The remaining questions of section 3 (items 3.5 to 3.9), which are not included in and reported for the index of academic confidence, indicate that race or institution is the single most important predictor variable in determining students' responses (3.5 institution, 3.6 race, 3.7 institution, 3.9 race).

The specific proportion of students' responses for item 3.5 reveal the following pattern: PT 49 per cent, CT 47 per cent, UWC 36 per cent, UCT 36 per cent and US 32 per cent. This indicates that students at the technikons are more likely to ask questions in class when they do not understand anything compared to the universities. For item 3.6 the figures reveal that white students (51%), then equally coloured and African students (46%), are more likely to ask lecturers questions when they do not understand anything pertaining to the subject. Item 3.9 shows that white students (51%) rely more on their own experiences than black students (African 45%, coloured 43%).

The analysis of item 3.7 reveals the following institutional pattern: UCT and US (72%), UWC (57%), CT (71%) and PT (65%). Thus, students at the three HAIs feel more confident to approach a librarian for help.

The results for item 3.8 suggest that home language is the most important variable. The specific results indicate that Afrikaans-speaking students (57%), then English-speaking students (55%) followed by speakers of African languages (47%), prefer to work on their own.

Index of reading and writing ability[3]

The index of reading and writing ability is based on responses to items 4.1 to 4.5 of the questionnaire. This index measures the reading and writing abilities and difficulties of students at the five institutions. The analysis of the results suggests that race and the index of confidence, that is, the confidence and motivation levels of students, are the most important predictor variables in explaining the pattern of the responses. This holds true for even those items of the section which are not included in the index of reading and writing ability.

The CHAID results indicate that for items 4.1 and 4.2 race is the most important predictor variable. The responses to item 4.1 indicate that more African (89%) than white students (70%)

"... students at the technikons are more likely to ask questions in class when they do not understand anything compared to the universities."

found prescribed reading difficult to understand often or sometimes. Of concern is the fact that only about 13 per cent of black (African and coloured) students did not experience difficulties in understanding prescribed readings. A similar pattern emerged with respect to item 4.2 referring to being given too many readings (African 87%, coloured 78%, white 61%).

Students' confidence emerged as the single most important predictor variable for items 4.3 to 4.5. Thus, for example, students' ability to structure an essay or assignment is, not surprisingly, conditioned by their levels of confidence and motivation as reported in the index of confidence. For example, the results indicate that more confident and active learners do not experience much difficulty in expressing "another writer's ideas in their own words" compared to those who are not confident and active learners.

The results for item 4.6, which is not included in the results of the index of reading and writing ability indicate that students' ability to prepare references or bibliographies is related to institution. The pattern that emerges is as follows: UCT (89% of the proportion of students), US (82%) and UWC, CT and PT (76%). While the differences in percentage terms are not large, the results indicate that students at the two technikons and two HDIs are less able to prepare references compared to students at UCT and US.

Index of computer competence[4]

"... students' ability to structure an essay or assignment is, not surprisingly, conditioned by their levels of confidence and motivation ..."

The index of computer competence is based on the responses to items 4.7 to 4.14. Predictor variables for these questions varied. The single most important predictor variables are race (items 4.7, 4.12 and 4.14), disciplinary domain (items 4.9, 4.10 and 4.13), institution (item 4.8) and gender (item 4.11).

The results for items 4.7, 4.12 and 4.14 indicate that knowledge of and competence in understanding the basis of computer work and advanced computer applications such as SPSS is strongly related to the race of students. Thus, for item 4.7, 80 per cent of white students compared to 54 per cent of African students are able to understand and effectively use/have some experience of computer operating systems such as Windows. The results for item 4.12 reveal that 18 per cent of white students, 14 per cent of African students and 10 per cent of coloured students are able to use mathematical and statistical packages. Thus, fewer students are familiar with advanced computer packages. Concerning multimedia packages (item 4.14) the results indicate that white students (34%) have more experience of these than black students (Indian 20%, coloured 19%, African 18%).

Disciplinary domain explains the patterns of responses to items 4.9, 4.10 and 4.13. In other words, students' subject specialisation is related to whether they are able to use a spreadsheet package, a database package or a package for CAD. This is not a surprising result as the teaching and utilisation of these packages are subject-specific. In this respect, the disciplines of natural science, engineering as well as economic and management sciences record the highest figures for students who are able to utilise these packages. For example, the result for item 4.9 indicates that students in the natural sciences (50%) are more familiar and have more experience with a spreadsheet package than those in the humanities (26%).

The ability to use a word-processing package is related to the institution where students study. The results indicate that for item 4.8, 84 per cent of CT students, followed by 79 per cent of UCT students, then 71 per cent of PT students, 68 per cent of US students and finally 52 per cent of UWC students can use a word-processing package.

For item 4.11, gender is the most important predictor variable in determining whether students are able to competently use a graphics programme. The results indicate that a greater proportion of males (31%) than females (18%) are able to use graphics programmes.

With respect to computer access in general (item 4.15) the institution is the most important predictor variable in accounting for the responses. The pattern of usage indicates that 78 per cent of UCT students, 73 per cent of US students, 44 per cent of UWC students, 79 per cent of CT students and 57 per cent of PT students have access to computers. This result indicates that more students at three HAIs have access to computers compared to students at the two HDIs, with UWC faring the worst.

Item 4.15i probed students with respect to whether they obtained access to the computers at their institution or not. CHAID analysis for this question indicates that home language is the first predictor variable that related to the pattern of student responses. Thus, 87 per cent of speakers of African languages compared to 65 per cent English-speaking students and 42 per cent Afrikaans-speaking students said that they relied on the institutions for access to computers. Thus, it can be inferred that African students in particular are heavily dependent on the universities and technikons for computer access.

With respect to e-mail access (item 4.16), the institution is the single most important variable that explained whether students had e-mail access or not. In this respect, 35 per cent of students at UCT and US, seven per cent of students at UWC, 36 per cent of students at CT and six per cent of students at PT had access to e-mail. Thus, students at the three HAIs reported far greater e-mail access than those at the two HDIs.

Item 4.16i attempted to ascertain whether such access is at the institution or whether students are able to privately and independently obtain e-mail access. The institution is here again the most important source of access with 72 per cent of UCT students, 85 per cent of US students, 37 per cent of UWC students, 61 per cent of CT students and 32 per cent of students claiming that they had access to the e-mail on their campuses.

"... 87 per cent of speakers of African languages compared to 65 per cent English-speaking students and 42 per cent Afrikaans-speaking students said that they relied on the institutions for access to computers."

Students' access to the Internet (item 4.17) is also related to institutional location. In other words, students' responses to whether they had Internet access or not is related to their institutional location. In this respect 38 per cent of UCT students, 32 per cent of US students, 12 per cent of UWC students, 41 per cent of CT students and 10 per cent of PT students state that they are able to access the Internet. The results indicate that students at the three HAIs have more access to the Internet than those at the HDIs.

On campus access (item 4.17i) is related to disciplinary domains. Thus, 69 per cent of economics and management students have access to the Internet on campus, compared to 57 per cent of students in the disciplinary domain of the natural sciences and humanities equally (57%).

Items 4.17ii, iii, iv, v and vi probed the usage of the Internet. In general, the results indicate that the reasons for the use of the Internet is explained by institutional location. Thus, whether students use the Internet to obtain information depends on their institutional location. The results for item 4.17ii indicate that UCT students (75%) are more likely to use the Internet for information compared to, for example, students at PT (52%). The pattern for item 4.17iii indicates that UCT students are more likely to use the Internet to make contact than any of the other institutions. The results for item 4.17iv suggests that more males (42%) than females (22%) use the Internet to download files. Responses to item 4.17v indicate that more coloured and Indian students (42%) followed by African students (32%) and then white students (21%) use the Internet to play games.

Items 4.18 to 4.20 asked students to indicate whether they have received academic-development and library training or not. The results indicate that for item 4.18 more African (43%) and coloured (23%) students than white (17%) students have attended academic-development programmes.

In respect of training in library orientation (item 4.19) the result suggests that a greater proportion of females (71%) than males (62%) have attended library-orientation sessions.

The results for advanced library instruction indicate that language is the most important variable in explaining student responses. Thus, those whose home language is an African language (30%), followed by English (16%) and then Afrikaans (13%), attended advanced library instruction. The results on language as a proxy for race suggest that more African students attended advanced library instruction than the other groups.

Index of library usage[5]

An important aspect of the questionnaire in determining the state of information literacy is to measure the extent to which students use the library. In particular, questions relating to library usage also attempted to ascertain the purposes for which students use the library. The index of library usage is constructed on the basis of the responses to items 4.21 to 4.30. In constructing the index, as mentioned previously, items 4.25, 4.27 and 4.30 are omitted based on the results of the factor analysis.

The CHAID results for the items that constitute the index of library usage indicate that race, institution and disciplinary domains are the single most important predictor variables.

Race is the single most important one in explaining the pattern of responses to items 4.23, 4.24 and 4.28. These questions focused on students finding readings from sources such as abstracts and bibliographies. In general, black (African, coloured and Indian) students are likely to use the library more often (once per week or month) than white students. The results for item 4.23 indicate that 56 per cent of African students used abstracts, indexes or bibliographies to find required reading once per month or more often, and 42 per cent of coloured and Indian students did likewise, compared to 27 per cent of the white-student sample. A similar picture was obtained for items 4.24 and 4.28. Specifically for item 4.24 the CHAID results indicate 61 per cent of African students, 41 per cent of coloured and Indian students and 29 per cent of white students look for reading from references once per month or more often. This picture holds true for item 4.28. It is thus the case that black students and African students in particular are, in respect of these three questions, frequent library users compared to their white counterparts.

"... the most frequent users of short loan/reserve collection are humanities and social sciences students compared with, for example, economic and management science students."

According to the results for items 4.22, 4.26 and 4.29, the institutional location of the students is the most single important predictor variable that accounts for the pattern of the responses. For item 4.22, the institutional location of the sample indicates the following results: UCT (66%), US (44%), UWC (73%), CT (68%) and PT (85%). This indicates that UWC and CT students are more frequent users of the open-shelf collections at the libraries than students at the other three institutions. The results for item 4.26 yield the following: UCT (73%), US (48%), UWC (59%), CT (68%) and PT (64%). These results indicate that students at UWC and PT are less familiar with computerised catalogues than those at the other three institutions. The result for item 4.29 reveals that 52 per cent of UCT students, 29 per cent of US students, 53 per cent of UWC students, 51 per cent of CT students and 58 per cent of PT students find useful material that is not specifically recommended. Of note is the low-percentage score for US students and the fairly high scores for UWC and PT.

Disciplinary domain explains the pattern of short loan/reserve collection usage (item 4.21). Not surprisingly, the most frequent users of short loan/reserve collection are humanities (84%) and social sciences (66%) students compared with, for example, economic and management science students (53%).

For items 4.25 (race), 4.27 (institution) and 4.30 (institution),

"... institution and race are the two most significant predictor variables in explaining the patterns and purposes of library usage by students ..."

which are not included in the index of library usage, race and institution are the two most important predictor variables. The result for item 4.25 indicates the following percentage figures by race group: African (34%), coloured (19%) and white (13%). Thus, more black students use the card catalogue than white. This is a surprising result as the card catalogue is not widely used at the five institutions. Percentage figures for item 4.27 indicate the following institutional pattern in relation to usage of CD-ROMs in the library: UCT (18%), US (12%), UWC (13%), CT and PT (16%). Of note here is the fact that students at the two technikons report to be fairly familiar with CD-ROMs compared to two of three universities. The following institutional pattern is revealed in relation to finding sources of information outside their own libraries: UCT (27%), US (20%), UWC and CT (40%) and PT (50%). This result is interesting in that it indicates that students at the two HDIs *and* those at the two technikons look for information outside their own institution's library.

In general, the picture that emerges is that institution and race are the two most significant predictor variables in explaining the patterns and purposes of library usage by students at the five higher-education institutions in the province. The results indicate that at the two HDIs, where the majority of students are mainly black, students are more likely to seek readings not prescribed. It possibly indicates a greater library culture at the two institutions and suggests that students at UWC and PT are more independent library users. While the reasons for this are not known, it is however clear that library usage features more strongly at the two HDIs.

Index of information needs[6]

The index of information needs is based on the responses to items 4.31 to 4.42. The index is divided into three sub-indexes. These are the index of basic information needs, index of basic computer-related needs and index of advanced computer-related needs.

In respect of basic information needs (reading and writing), the results indicate that race is the most important predictor variable in accounting for items 4.31 to 4.33. For item 4.31, 85 and 77 per cent of African and coloured students respectively often/sometimes require help with writing essays and assignments compared to 61 per cent of white students. The results for item 4.32 reveal the following pattern: African (77%), coloured (69%), Indian (60%) and white (45%), so that fewer white than black students in general often/sometimes have difficulty in understanding references on reading lists. More black students (African 68%, coloured 66%, Indian 58%) than white students (46%) require help with compiling references and bibliographies (item 4.33). With respect to requiring guidance in finding things in the library (item 4.34) the results indicate that about 85 per cent of all students frequently/sometimes need help (UCT 80%, US 80%, UWC 86%), CT and PT 78%). Of note is the fact that the two technikons yield the same results.

For items 4.35 to 4.37 (index of basic computer-related needs) race again emerges as the single most important predictor variable. The results for training in the use of computer word-processing (item 4.35) indicate that 77 per cent of African students, followed by 76 per cent of coloured and Indian students and then 30 per cent of white students, require help often/sometimes. More coloured and Indian (75%) and African students (68%) indicate a need for training in the uses of computer-spreadsheet software (item 4.36) compared to white students (63%). It is important that the differences in percentage terms are not that large across all race groups. The results for item 4.37 show a similar pattern to that of item 4.46, though the percentage figures are slightly different.

Similar to the results of the index of basic computer-related needs above, race is once more the most important predictor variable in explaining the index of advanced computer-related needs. The results for item 4.38 indicate that 67 per cent of coloured students and 59 per cent of African students compared to 55 per cent of white students express a need (often/sometimes) for training in the use of a graphics programme such as Harvard Graphics. More black students in general (Indian 68%, coloured 61%, African 57%) compared to white students (45%) express a need for training in the use of mathematical or statistical analysis packages such as SPSS (item 4.39). Similarly, for item 4.40 more black students (coloured 68%, African 62%) express a need for training in the use of computer-aided design packages such as CAD. The difference in need by race is found in 4.41, where 81 per cent of coloured and 80 per cent of white students express a need for training in the use of the Internet, compared to 65 per cent of African students.

With the exception of item 4.34, race is the single most important predictor variable for the items of the questionnaire and indexes relating to information needs. More specifically, it is mainly black students in general, and African students in particular, who for most of the questions (barring 4.41) often/sometimes require help and training in various aspects of computer-related information-literacy skills and competencies. The results thus indicate that black students in general are the most in need of support and training to acquire the basic skills needed to become information literate. Furthermore, the results indicate that competencies in the various aspects of information literacy identified in the questionnaire is related to race.

The results for the items relating to the index of information needs are strongly related to the index of computer competence, where race and institution are the single most significant predictor variables for students' computer competence. Analysis of the results for the two indexes suggests that black students are least computer-competent and are in most need of help and training on aspects of information use.

Index of independent learning[7]

As mentioned previously, the index of independent learning is based on responses to section 5 of the questionnaire (items 5.1 to 5.10). Three indexes comprise the index of independent learning. These are the index of interactive learning (items 5.2, 5.3, 5.4 and 5.8), the index of individual learning (items 5.1, 5.5, 5.6 and 5.7) and the index of media-based learning (items 5.9 and 5.10).

The results indicate that, for the items that comprise the index of interactive learning, disciplinary domain is the single most important predictor variable. For item 5.2, the results indicate that across most disciplinary domains students worked in small groups. The differences between disciplinary domains are marginal in percentage terms. Somewhat unexpectedly, the results for item 5.2 indicate that it is the medical and health sciences (74%), followed by engineering and design sciences (61%), where students do field work outside the institution. Humanities students (37%) are comparatively less likely to engage in fieldwork. The disciplinary-domain pattern that emerges for item 5.4 reveals that more natural sciences and engineering students (95%) as well as medical and health sciences students (92%) are likely to engage in practical assignments compared to humanities (66%) and social sciences (79%). In general, the picture that emerges is that the more applied disciplines are likely to engage in the forms of learning associated with the index of independent interactive learning.

The only exception to the pattern refers to responses to item 5.8 where the results indicate that race is the single most important predictor variable. Thus, it is African (74%) and coloured (62%) students who are more often likely to interview other people to obtain information (item 5.8) than their white counterparts (54%). This result indicates that the extent to which students rely on other people for information support and assistance is related to race.

The results for the index of individual learning indicate that disciplinary domain is the single most important predictor variable for items 5.1 and 5.5. As expected, for item 5.1 it is the disciplinary domains of humanities (99%) and social sciences (86%) where students are most often likely to write essays compared to the discipline of the natural sciences (68%). The frequency with which students watched videos/films that are recommended (item 5.5) indicates that those from the disciplines of the humanities (72%) and medical and health sciences (68%) are most likely to do so often/sometimes. It is interesting to note that this practice happens least in the social sciences (54%).

Not surprisingly, students' ability to present oral views contrary to those of other students' or lecturers' (item 5.6) is related to their scores on the index of confidence. Thus, students who are highly confident and active learners (81%) are often/sometimes more likely to present contrary views than those who lacked confidence and felt disengaged from the learning process (50%). It is thus the case that students' ability to articulate different positions is related to the extent to which the teaching and learning process empowers and engages them. This implies that the pedagogic process should create the conditions to make students become confident and active learners.

Institutional location is the single most important predictor variable for item 5.7. In this respect, the results reveal the following pattern: UCT (73%), US (58%), UWC and PT (79%) and PT (84%). Thus students at the two technikons and the two HDIs are most likely to find relevant reading without the help of a reading list. Of note here is that students at US are least likely to find relevant readings without the help of a reading list.

The extent to which students obtain information from other media such as radio, TV and newspapers is best explained by the variables of race and disciplinary domains. The results for item 5.10 reveal the following breakdown of results by race: African (84%), coloured (78%), Indian (72%), white (65%). Thus, black students in general are often more likely to rely on the radio and TV to obtain information than white students. The frequent reliance on newspapers to find information is best explained by disciplinary domain (item 5.11). The results reveal the following pattern of newspaper usage by discipline: humanities (84%), social sciences (90%), natural sciences (72%), economic and management sciences (80%). This result is not surprising.

In general, disciplinary domain emerges as the most important predictor variable for the majority of items that constitute the section on independent learning. Thus, the extent to which students are encouraged to engage in different forms of independent learning activities relates to the discipline within which they specialise. This implies that more attention has to be paid to the pedagogic approaches within disciplines and subjects if, at the higher-education level, academics wish to create independent learners.

"It is thus the case that students' ability to articulate different positions is related to the extent to which the teaching and learning process empowers and engages them."

Conclusion[8]

This chapter has highlighted and discussed the key predictor variables which explain the differences in responses for each item of the questionnaire.

As Table 6.1 indicates, a key finding to emerge is the fact that race, institutional location and disciplinary domain are the single most important predictor variables which account for the results obtained. A number of noteworthy features are apparent.

Firstly, three key variables, namely race, institution and disciplinary domain respectively explain the variances in the responses to most of the questions. Notably, "race" explains 40 per cent of the responses to the items of the questionnaire, and "institution" accounts for 28 per cent of the responses to the questionnaire items.

Secondly, the results indicate important racial and institutional differences in the region. Concerning the former, the results suggest that black students in general are less competent and most in need of different aspects of information literacy. In respect of institution, the results suggest that students at UWC and PT have less access to computer- and other facilities than those at UCT, US and CT.

Thirdly, the analysis of the index of confidence reveals interesting differences. While white students are more confident in respect of leadership and working on their own, the results indicate that black students in general and students at the two technikons are more willing to ask lecturers questions in and after class.

Fourthly, an interesting feature of the results is the pattern of library usage. The results indicate that students at UWC and PT are more likely to be frequent library users engaged in, inter alia, looking for readings that are not prescribed.

TABLE 6.1: Summary of predictor variables for questionnaire items

Variable	Number of occurrences	Question numbers
Race	27	3.1, 3.4, 3.6, 3.9 4.1, 4.2, 4.7, 4.12, 4.14, 4.17 v, 4.18, 4.23, 4.24, 4.25, 4.28, 4.31, 4.32, 4.33, 4.35, 4.36, 4.37, 4.38, 4.39, 4.40, 4.41, 5.8, 5.9
Institution	19	3.2, 3.3, 3.5, 3.7 4.6, 4.8, 4.15 I, 4.16, 4.16 I, 4.17, 4.17 ii, 4.17 iii, 4.22, 4.26, 4.27, 4.29, 4.30, 4.34 5.7
Disciplinary domain	11	4.9, 4.10, 4.13, 4.17 I, 4.21 5.1, 5.2, 5.3, 5.4, 5.5, 5.10
Gender	4	4.11, 4.17 iv, 4.14 vi, 4.19
Confidence index	4	4.3, 4.4, 4.5 5.6
Language	3	3.8 4.15, 4.20

Notes

[1] A detailed output of the results obtained from the CHAID analysis is available from the INFOLIT offices.

[2] For all five- point scales of the questionnaire, the results reported combined responses 1 and 2, and 4 and 5. Thus, results at the extreme ends of the scale are combined.

[3] The results for the items of this index are based on a three-point scale (often, sometimes, never). In reporting the results, the categories of often and sometimes are combined.

4   The items for this question are based on a four-point scale (competent users, some experienced but not competent, unable to use but would like to, unable to use and do not want to). In reporting the results, the first two points of the scale (competent users, some experience but not competent) are combined. The last two categories of the scale are kept separate.

5   The item for the index of library usage uses a four-point scale (1 = once per week, 2 = once per month, 3 = once per semester, 4 = never or hardly ever). In reporting the results, the percentage figures for 1 and 2 of the scales are combined.

6   The results for the items of the index are based on a three-point scale (often, sometimes, never). In reporting the results, the categories of often and sometimes are combined.

7   The results for the items of the index are based on a three-point scale (often, sometimes, never). In reporting the results, the categories of often and sometimes are combined.

8   In interpreting the results of the CHAID analysis, it is important to note that race and institution are often correlated in that the majority of students at some institutions are black. Thus, what is sometimes institutions may reflect race and *vice versa*.

7

Synopsis of Findings and Recommendations

The study represents an important first step in obtaining a profile of the information-literacy skills of students at the five tertiary institutions in the region. It has provided both institutional profiles as well as a regional profile. It has highlighted students' responses to key aspects of information literacy, namely confidence, reading and writing ability, computer competence, library usage, information needs and independent learning.

This study is based upon the definition and discussion of information literacy in chapter 2. To recap, the definition reads as follows:

> Information literacy refers to the ability of learners to access, use and evaluate information from different sources, in order to enhance learning, solve problems and generate new knowledge.

The study is framed in a context in which higher-education institutions and students have had different and unequal resources and opportunities as a consequence of the system of apartheid education. The working definition of information literacy indicates that in the South African context, information literacy must take due cognisance of the prior learning experiences and contextually specific teaching and learning practices. Given this understanding, an important aspect of this study relates the dimensions of information literacy contained in the definition to variables of learning pertinent to the South African context. These include year level, language, race, institution, disciplinary domain, gender, academic performance and age.

This section lists the findings of the study. The conclusions prominently display the historical legacy that the South African higher-education system has inherited and is currently challenged to transform. The importance of race as a key variable in understanding information literacy in the region reflects the pervasive influence of the policies of the past on the present as institutions grapple with the future.

Confidence

The definition of information literacy as discussed in Chapter 2 of the book indicates that confidence and motivation of learners is a key characteristic of an information-literate person. This dimension displays the following three key features. Firstly, the results indicate that white students are more confident than black students to act as leaders and to take initiative. It would be important to further investigate the factors that lead to this. Secondly, the result suggests that black students and students at the two technikons are more confident to engage with lecturers in- and outside the classroom. Finally, the results indicate that white students rely more on their life experiences and they prefer to work on their own compared to black students. This suggests that black students have a greater disposition toward group work.

However, an important aspect of the findings is that the confidence expressed by black students in respect of engaging with lecturers does not translate into competence in different aspects of information literacy, for example, with regard to academic literacy and computer competence.

Computer competence

An important part of the study was to ascertain the competence of students in respect of three areas of information literacy, namely reading and writing ability, library usage and computer competence.

The findings of the study suggest that at least a third of all students express reading and writing difficulties. Specific problems that were identified are the ability to express writers' ideas in their own words and that less confident students are those who experience more reading and writing difficulties. The results suggest that black students (African, coloured and Indian) experience more difficulties than white students in respect of understanding and coping with the amount of readings they are given.

The results of the index of computer competence indicate that familiarity and computer competence are strongly related to race and disciplinary domain. The results indicate that in general black students are less familiar and competent with computers than their white counterparts. As expected, the results suggest that in specific areas of computing, such as CAD, students in the natural and applied sciences (engineering) indicate that they are more competent. The interesting feature of the results was the issue of access to computers and facilities such as e-mail and the Internet. The results indicate that students at UWC and PT have less access to computers and such facilities than their counterparts at UCT, US and CT. This confirms differences between the HDIs and HAIs in respect of resources. Moreover, the results indicate that for those who have access to these facilities, black students in general rely on their institution for access. This implies that black students have less private access to computers and such facilities as the Internet.

"The results indicate that students at UWC and PT have less access to computers and such facilities than their counterparts at UCT, US and CT. This confirms differences between the HDIs and HAIs in respect of resources."

Library usage

The results for the index of library usage reveal an interesting picture. The study's findings indicate that black students and those at UWC and PT report positively on most of the aspects relating to library usage. Thus, more black than white students engage in library activities such as looking for readings other than those prescribed. It is also the case that students at UWC and PT engage in independent library usage such as finding relevant material that was not prescribed. The general impression is that black students and students at UWC and PT make extensive use of the library for finding sources of information that are not prescribed. The study thus indicates that students at UWC and PT use the library much more independently than those at UCT, US and CT. The critical question which requires further investigation is, how such information is evaluated and utilised.

Information needs

All three indexes of information needs (index of basic information need, index of computer-related needs and index of advanced computer-related needs) indicate that for the majority of items that measure information needs, race accounts for most of the differences recorded. The results show that a greater proportion of black students express need in all the areas of information-literacy activities such as reading and writing and computer usage than their white counterparts. The results, particularly for the index of basic information needs, are strongly related to the results for the index of reading and writing ability and the index of computer competence.

"... more black than white students engage in library activities such as looking for readings other than those prescribed."

Independent learning

The results of the study suggest that for most of the items that make up the three indexes of independent learning (index of interactive learning, index of individual learning and index of media-based learning), disciplinary domain is the most significant factor. Thus the forms of independent learning in which students engage are related to differences between disciplinary domains. Consequently, students in the applied disciplines (for example, engineering and design) are more likely to undertake fieldwork and practical assignments, while students in the humanities and social sciences are more involved in learning activities such as writing essays.

Information literacy and performance

While the CHAID analysis does not indicate performance as a first predictor variable, the comparative analysis of results by institutions (Chapter 6) reveals a strong relationship between performance and the various indexes of information literacy. These results resonate with the findings of a study (Brake 1997: 5) which suggests that students able to interact positively with new information technologies perform better academically. This result suggests that improved performance might be related to better information-literacy skills. This is certainly an area of research that warrants further investigation.

Information literacy and race

It has already been mentioned that racial differences feature strongly in the information-literacy abilities and skills of students in the Western Cape region. The results of chapters 5 and 6 strongly suggest that the race of students is important in explaining the degree of information literacy they possess. Concerning the notion of information literacy discussed in Chapter 2, black students feel less able to access and use information and consequently express greater need for information-literacy development.

Information literacy and gender

The comparative institutional analyses (see Chapter 6) suggest that for some aspects of information literacy there are important gender differences. In instances of these, the results reveal that females indicate less competence and greater need than their male counterparts. Thus, for example, a greater proportion of female students report lower levels of confidence and less competence in computer usage.

Information literacy and disciplinary domain

It is evident that many aspects of information literacy are strongly related to disciplinary domain. Chapter 6 indicates that disciplinary domain is the most significant predictor variable for 11 items of the questionnaire. These items cluster mainly into aspects of computer usage and, more importantly, questions relating to forms of independent learning. Thus, the results for the questions relating to independent learning suggest that the extent to which students engage in forms of independent learning is related to disciplinary domain.

Information literacy and year level

The findings of the study indicate that there is no obvious relation between year group and information-literacy abilities and needs. This is perhaps due to the fact that the sample size for the year groups across the institution was uneven. Nonetheless, the results tentatively suggest that senior students, that is, third- and fourth-year students, are less competent computer users than the junior undergraduates. It is also interesting to note that students reporting competence in aspects of information literacy such as reading and writing decrease across the year levels.

Information literacy and age

The age variable indicates a strong relationship with information-literacy abilities and needs. Older students report, for example, more frequent library usage as well as greater levels of engaging in forms of independent learning.

In general, students' information-literacy needs and abilities in the region share the following characteristics:

- Race features strongly in students' information-literacy abilities and needs. On average, black students express less competence in aspects of information literacy and consequently greater need. This suggests that in the South African context, prior learning experiences and the educational backgrounds of students are critical in understanding their information-literacy abilities and needs.
- Institutional location is an important variable in explaining the pattern of information literacy in the region. Thus, institutional location explains access to information sources, forms of pedagogy, patterns of library usage and information needs. The variable of institutional location indicates both the differences between universities and technikons, and between UCT, US and CT, and UWC and PT.
- Disciplinary domain is a key factor in understanding the state of information literacy in the region. Teaching and learning approaches within specific domains shape information-literacy characteristics in learners.
- Students who report high academic performance scores also indicate greater competence and consequently less need in the aspects of information literacy identified in the questionnaire.

"The starting point of information-literacy activities must therefore be the resources that students bring with them, with due attention to the learning contexts from which they come and enter into."

Recommendations

The following recommendations are made which, it is hoped, will provide some ideas for taking the results of the study forward.

Recommendation 1: Consider students' prior learning experiences

The study suggests that students' information-literacy abilities and needs are shaped by their prior learning experiences and education backgrounds. Thus a key recommendation is that, in planning information-literacy activities, the learning backgrounds of students need to be taken into account. This implies that such programmes should focus on providing students who have been disadvantaged by previous policies with the necessary information-literacy skills to participate equally in the changing forms of learning. The starting point of information-literacy activities must therefore be the resources that students bring with them, with due attention to the learning contexts from which they come and enter into.

Recommendation 2: Change schooling practices

The study highlights the influence of prior learning in students' information-literacy abilities and needs. In the context of this study, part of the prior learning experience relates to teaching and learning approaches at the school level. This specifically implies the need to develop information-literacy abilities at the school level. A key recommendation is the need to transform the schooling contexts of the majority of disadvantaged students in this country in order to ensure that students who enter the higher-education system are equipped with the necessary information-literacy competencies. This recommendation resonates with the emphasis of the Green Paper on Higher Education on transforming the schooling system to enable more prepared learners to enter higher education.

Recommendation 3: Provide the necessary infrastructure for information literacy

It is apparent from the study that the acquisition of information-literacy skills critically hinges upon basic infrastructure, such as computers being in place at the institutional level. The study indicates that this is not the case, particularly at the two HDIs. Thus, the two HDIs must be enabled to obtain the basic minimum infrastructural support that is necessary for the spread of information-literacy activities.

A specific recommendation of the study in this respect is that earmarked funding be obtained through and with the support of various agencies, inter alia, the Infolit project, the government and donor agencies. Institutions should, in turn, develop a vision and strategy that actively supports such funding activities.

Together with the basic minimum physical infrastructure, it is important to have academics who are aware and able to integrate the new information technologies to promote student-centred learning.

"... the acquisition of information-literacy skills critically hinges upon basic infrastructure, such as computers being in place at the institutional level."

Recommendation 4: Targeted information-literacy programmes and activities

A high proportion of all students indicate a lack of competence and consequently a great need in the dimensions of information literacy that the questionnaire is based upon. This, as the results indicate, cuts across all racial groups. However, black students express less competence and more need. This implies the need for information-literacy programmes and activities which address the needs identified in the study and attend to the levels of competence found for all students, with particular emphasis on black students.

Recommendation 5: Share programmes, resources and facilities

It is implied in the previous recommendation that greater collaboration and co-operation is vital in providing what is obviously a concern of all five institutions, namely graduating information-literate students. Collaborative ventures could include activities such as sharing of resources and delivery of common information-literacy courses. Collaboration within this framework implies improving the quality of learning for all, so that expertise is spread across the system. This would entail the systematic and systemic restructuring of *ad hoc* initiatives into transferable and adaptable programmes.

Recommendation 6: Change pedagogy

It is apparent that information-literacy needs become a much greater part of higher-education institutions. This suggests offering information-literacy programmes across all disciplines and subjects. It also suggests moving toward greater resource-based learning. To institutionalise information literacy, pedagogical approaches at the higher-education level need to change to a student-centred approach which enables learners to become independent. Thus, it is important for the five institutions to consider information-literacy programmes to develop the necessary information-literacy skills. This involves changing mainstream practices to ensure that existing courses display a greater information-literacy orientation. This could include courses where students are actively encouraged to seek information from the range of information sources that are available and are enabled to critically use these skills.

Changing pedagogy is understandably a process which occurs over a lengthy period of time. Thus, changes towards resource-based learning and enhanced information literacy will require long-term institutional commitments.

"To institutionalise information literacy, pedagogical approaches at the higher-education level need to change to a student-centred approach which enables learners to become independent."

Recommendation 7: Audit best practice

This study has provided base-line results on the state of information literacy in the region. It has been mainly based on students' perceptions of their information-literacy abilities and needs. To enrich the study, it is necessary to undertake an investigation of those teaching practices that advance information-literacy education. A central aspect of such an investigation should be to determine ways in which good information-literacy practices can be spread through the higher-education system.

Recommendation 8: Advocating and lobbying for information-literacy education

To create greater information-literacy awareness and consciousness, stronger lobbying and advocacy is necessary. The Infolit Project is a step in this direction. In addition, the international study visit has shown that for institutional culture to shift in the direction of greater information-literacy awareness, high-level endorsement and support is required. Thus, it is a task of senior management at the five institutions to argue for and provide information-literacy work through, for example, ensuring that the basic infrastructure to advance student-centred learning is in place. The support of the deputy vice-chancellors/rectors displayed throughout the course of this study is indicative of this.

The study has provided a general overview of students' information-literacy abilities and needs across the five institutions in the region. It has identified gaps and weaknesses in information-literacy provision. Yet, it has also shown positive learning in the region. However, caution needs to be exercised in drawing too hard and firm generalisations from the study, for what is reflected here is a snapshot which can only be elaborated with further research including, as indicated, a strong qualitative orientation. Perhaps the most important implication of the results is the need for more proactive, integrated and co-operative information-literacy programmes and activities.

8

Information Literacy: A Strategic Plan

This study was conceptualised as part of an overall strategy of transforming higher education towards resource-based, technology-enhanced learning, seeking to produce active and critical citizens able to meet the challenges of a modernising economy in a globally competitive environment. In this respect it has listed a number of recommendations. In order to operationalise these recommendations, a key step would be to produce a strategic implementation plan for information literacy.

A strategic implementation plan for information literacy has to be framed within a context of and with commitment to greater inter-institutional collaboration and co-operation exemplified by the activities of the WCTIT. Thus, a strategic implementation plan for information literacy would target information-literacy activities which allow for a sharing of resources, experiences and expertise across the five higher-education institutions in the Western Cape region. The model of co-operation manifest in the Calico Project is instructive in this respect.

There are two key areas to consider in developing a strategic implementation plan. Firstly, due attention must be paid to activities which promote information literacy in the region. This includes the following:

- ways of distributing the results of the study so that it can reach as wide an audience as possible and serve as a basis for discussion on advancing information-literacy education,
- providing an ongoing and sustainable forum for information-literacy dialogue and discussion,
- ways of identifying and spreading best information-literacy practices intra- and inter-institutionally,
- ways of interfacing with other academic-development initiatives aimed at enhancing teaching and learning,
- generating the necessary human-resource development to support and advance information-literacy education.

Secondly, there is a clear need for ongoing and systematic research concerning information literacy. In this respect, some of the research work that the Infolit project needs to consider includes:

- a programme evaluation study of the pilot projects. This would entail an assessment of their intended information-literacy outcomes. In addition, such a study would measure the extent to which the lessons from specific pilot projects can be extended to other institutions and other academic programmes;
- an in-depth, qualitatively orientated investigation of best information-literacy practices at the five higher-education institutions. This should include a comprehensive investigation of lecturers' perceptions of and initiatives towards enhancing students' information-literacy attributes. This study has produced some preliminary data and analysis in this regard which can serve as a valuable baseline for further investigations.

The publication of this study places Infolit in a position to engage stakeholders in a process of developing a strategic implementation plan which can give practical intent to the need for information literacy highlighted in the investigation.

Appendix

Questionnaire to Students on Information Literacy

University or Technikon Code: ☐ (1)

Faculty or School Code:. ☐☐ (2-3)

Subject Code: ☐☐ (4-5)

Year of Study or Level Code: ☐ (6)

Please answer the following questions to the best of your ability.

1   Please place a tick [√] in the appropriate box   *For Office Use*

1.1   Age: under 22   22 - 29   30 or older
              ☐ 1   ☐ 2   ☐ 3   ☐ (7)

1.2   Gender: Female   Male
                      ☐ 1   ☐ 2   ☐ (8)

1.3   Racial classification. By "racial classification" we are referring to those categories
       previously identified by the population registration acts.

       Black   White   Coloured   Indian
       ☐ 1   ☐ 2   ☐ 3   ☐ 4   ☐ (9)

1.4   On average, what have most of your results **in your major or intended major subjects**
       been this year? **Please place a tick [√] in the appropriate box.**

- 45%	45 - 49 %	50 -59 %	60 - 69 %	70 - 74%	+ 75%
1	2	3	4	5	6

☐ (10)

2.   Please place a tick [√] in the appropriate box

2.1   Which matric examining board was your school part of?

[1]	Cape	[6]	House of Delegates
[2]	Transvaal	[7]	DET
[3]	Natal	[8]	TBVC
[4]	Free State	[9]	Other
[5]	House of Representatives		

☐☐ (12 - 11)

1

2.2 What is your first language? **(Please tick [√] one box only)**

Afrikaans	1	S.Sotho	5	Xhosa	9
English	2	Swazi	6	Zulu	10
Ndebele	3	Tsonga	7	Venda	11
N.Sotho	4	Tswana	8	Other (please specify)	12

....

(13 - 14)

Please circle Yes or No

2.3 Did you receive your high school tuition through the medium of your
first language?

Y	N
[1]	[2]

(15)

2.4 Please name the TOWN and SCHOOL in which you matriculated:
Town:

....

(16 - 18)

High School:

....

(19 - 21)

3 *Please rate yourself on the scale as indicated below by placing a circle [O] on the number that most closely represents your position on the scale*

> **For example:**
> *I attend all the lectures, tutorials and other timetabled class meetings.*
> *I never go to class (1)   (2)   (3)   ④   (5)   I go to every single class*

3.1 I like to act as a leader for the group if a task has been assigned to my group
I'm always the leader   (1)   (2)   (3)   (4)   (5)   I hate taking the lead

(22)

3.2 I like to answer lecturers' questions in class
I'm the first to answer   (1)   (2)   (3)   (4)   (5)   I never know what to say

(23)

3.3 I speak up in class when students' opinions are asked
I'm the first to speak up   (1)   (2)   (3)   (4)   (5)   I never open my mouth

(24)

3.4 I am eager to tackle a challenging assignment
I can't wait to get started   (1)   (2)   (3)   (4)   (5)   I put it off until the last moment

(25)

3.5 I ask questions in class when I do not understand something
I hate to admit that I don't understand   (1)   (2)   (3)   (4)   (5)   I ask immediately

(26)

3.6 I ask my lecturer after class when I do not understand something
I'm too shy to approach a lecturer   (1)   (2)   (3)   (4)   (5)   I like talking to a lecturer

(27)

3.7 I ask a librarian for assistance when I need help in the library
Librarians are there to help students   (1)   (2)   (3)   (4)   (5)   Librarians are too busy to
be bothered

(28)

3.8. & 3.9 ☞

2

3.8   I participate in informal study groups that we arrange among our classmates

I prefer to work on my own   (1)   (2)   (3)   (4)   (5)   I work best with my classmates

☐
(29)

3.9   I rely on my own life experiences to help me cope with learning demands in
      tertiary education

I know that I can find out by
myself what I need to know   (1)   (2)   (3)   (4)   (5)   I rely on the experiences of my
                                                                      group to find out what we need

☐
(30)

4   Please place a tick [√] in the appropriate box.

	Often	Sometimes	Never	
4.1 I find prescribed readings difficult to understand	1	2	3	☐ (31)
4.2 I am given too many readings with which to cope.	1	2	3	☐ (32)
4.3 I have difficulty in expressing my own ideas.	1	2	3	☐ (33)
4.4 I have difficulty in expressing another writer's idea in my own words.	1	2	3	☐ (34)
4.5 I find it difficult to structure an essay or assignment	1	2	3	☐ (35)
4.6 I am able to prepare a list of references or bibliographies to attach to my written work.	1	2	3	☐ (36)

Please place a tick [√] in the appropriate box

How many kinds of computer software packages are you able to use?

Please rate your **competence** on a scale of:
        1 = **I am able** to use this kind of package competently/confidently
        2 = I have **some experience**, but cannot use it competently/confidently
        3 = **I am unable** to use this kind of package, but **would like** to
        4 = **I am unable** to use this kind of package, but **do not need or want to:**

	1	2	3	4	
4.7 A computer operating system (e.g. MS-DOS or Windows)	1	2	3	4	☐ (37)
4.8 A word-processing package (e.g. MS-Word or Word-Perfect)	1	2	3	4	☐ (38)
4.9 A spreadsheet package (e.g. Excel or Lotus)	1	2	3	4	☐ (39)
4.10 A database package (e.g. Access or D-Base)	1	2	3	4	☐ (40)
4.11 A graphics programme (e.g. Harvard Graphics)	1	2	3	4	☐ (41)
4.12. A package for mathematical or statistical analysis (e.g. SPSS or SAS)	1	2	3	4	☐ (42)
4.13 A package for computer aided design (e.g. CAD)	1	2	3	4	☐ (43)
4.14 Multimedia packages on CD-ROM	1	2	3	4	☐ (44)

3

Please circle YES or NO

4.15   Do you currently have access to a computer for your own use?

Y N
[1] [2]

☐
(45)

If **Yes**, is this computer on campus?

Y N
[1] [2]

☐
(46)

4.16   Do you currently use electronic mail?

Y N
[1] [2]

☐
(47)

If **Yes**: do you use it on campus?

Y N
[1] [2]

☐
(48)

4.17   Do you currently have access to the **Internet**?

Y N
[1] [2]

☐
(49)

If Yes: do you use it on campus?

Y N
[1] [2]

☐
(50)

do you use it to obtain information?

Y N
[1] [2]

☐
(51)

do you use it to make contact with others?

Y N
[1] [2]

☐
(52)

do you use it to download files?

Y N
[1] [2]

☐
(53)

do you use it to play games?

Y N
[1] [2]

☐
(54)

any other uses? Please specify.

Y N
[1] [2]

☐☐
(55 -56)

....

Please circle Yes or No.

4.18   Have you attended a course on **study skills** at your institution

Y N
[1] [2]

☐
(57)

4.19   Have you attended a **library orientation** session at your institution?

Y N
[1] [2]

☐
(58)

4.20   Have you attended more **advanced** library instruction sessions
on specific finding tools and skills?

Y N
[1] [2]

☐
(59)

4

Please place a tick [√] in the appropriate box.

Please rate how many of the following have you used or done **at the library** in your institution
according to the following scale:

  1 = once per **week** or more often
  2 = once per **month** or more often
  3 = once per **semester** or more often
  4 = **never** or hardly ever.

Your rating

					For Office Use
4.21	Used the short **loan/reserve** collection in the library find required readings	1 2 3 4			(60)
4.22	Used the **open shelves** to find relevant readings	1 2 3 4			(61)
4.23	Used **abstracts, indexes** or **bibliographies** to find required readings	1 2 3 4			(62)
4.24	Looked for **other readings** from references found in articles that you have read	1 2 3 4			(63)
4.25	Used the **card catalogue** in the library	1 2 3 4			(64)
4.26	Used the **computerised** catalogue in the library	1 2 3 4			(65)
4.27	Used **CD-ROM's** in the library	1 2 3 4			(66)
4.28	Asked a librarian for help	1 2 3 4			(67)
4.29	Found useful/relevant material that was not specifically prescribed	1 2 3 4			(68)
4.30	While at this institution, used information sources outside the library to find material related to your course work.(please specify)	1 2 3 4			(69a)

....

....

(69b)

Please place a tick [√] in the appropriate box.

Have you ever felt a need for any of the following at your institution?

		Often	Sometimes	Never	
4.31	Help with writing essays or assignments	1	2	3	(70)
4.32	Help with understanding references on reading lists	1	2	3	(71)
4.33	Help with compiling references or bibliographies	1	2	3	(72)
4.34	Guidance with finding things in the library	1	2	3	(73)
4.35	Training in the use of a computer word processing package (e.g. MS-Word or Word-Perfect).	1	2	3	(74)
4.36	Training in the use of computer spreadsheet software (e.g. Excel or Lotus).	1	2	3	(75)
4.37	Training in the use of computer data base software (e.g. Access or D-Base).	1	2	3	(76)

4.38 - 4.42 ↵

Please place a tick [√] in the appropriate box
Have you ever felt the need for any of the following at your institution?.

		Often	Sometimes	Never
4.38	Training in the use of a graphics program (e.g. Harvard Graphics)	1	2	3
4.39	Training in the use of a package for mathematical or statistical analysis (e.g. SPSS or SAS)	1	2	3
4.40	Training in the use of a package for computer aided design (e.g. CAD)	1	2	3
4.41	Training in the use of the Internet	1	2	3
4.42	Anything else (Please specify)	1	2	3

☐ (77)

☐ (78)

☐ (79)

☐ (80)

☐☐ (81-82a)

☐☐ (81-82b)

....

5   **Please place a tick [√] in the appropriate box.**

Which of the following have you done during the **past 6 months**?

		Often	Sometimes	Never
5.1	Written essays	1	2	3
5.2	Worked in small groups	1	2	3
5.3	Done fieldwork outside my institution	1	2	3
5.4	Done practical assignments	1	2	3
5.5	Looked at films or videos that were recommended/ prescribed in class	1	2	3
5.6	Orally presented a point of view that disagreed with that held by other students or the lecturer	1	2	3
5.7	Found relevant readings on my own without the help of reading lists	1	2	3
5.8	Interviewed other people for information	1	2	3
5.9	Watched TV or listened to the radio to find information	1	2	3
5.10	Read newspapers to find information	1	2	3
5.11	Found other sources of information (please specify)	1	2	3

☐ (83)

☐ (84)

☐ (85)

☐ (86)

☐ (87)

☐ (88)

☐ (89)

☐ (90)

☐ (91)

☐ (92)

☐ (93)

☐☐ (94-95)

....
....

6

***Please note below, or on the back of this sheet, any other comments
that you may have on any aspect of this questionnaire:***

_____

_____

_____

_____

_____

_____

_____

_____

_____

_____

_____

_____

_____

_____

_____

_____

_____

_____

_____

lease note your name, address and student number if you are willing to be interviewed
bout studying and learning at this institution:

Jame:_____

\ddress:_____

_____

_____

_____

_____

itudent Number:_____

`hank you very much for your co-operation.

Bibliography

Adams, S. and G. D. Bailey, 1993. "Education for the information age: Is it time to trade vehicles?" *NASSP Bulletin,* May: 57–63.

Behrens, S., 1992. "Thesis: Undergraduate library and information skills in a distance learning environment", unpublished doctoral thesis, University of South Africa.

—, 1993. "User education at tertiary level: A review of recent literature", *South African Journal of Library Science,* 61 (13): 124–130.

—, 1994. "A conceptual analysis and historical overview of information literacy." *College and Research Libraries,* July; 309–322.

Bodi, S., 1995. "Scholarship or propaganda: How can librarians help undergraduates tell the difference?" *The Journal of Academic Librarianship,* January.

Brake, D., 1997. "The net benefits of learning from home". *The New Scientist,* February.

Breivik, P. S., 1987. "Making the most of libraries". *Change.* 19 (4): 44–52.

Bruce, C. S., 1994. "Information literacy blueprint." Division of Information Services. Griffith University. [On-line].

—, 1995. "Information literacy: A framework for higher education". *The Australian Library Journal.* August: 158–170.

Cram, J., 1995. "A critical competence: Information literacy and the Australian experience". Paper delivered at the South African Institute of Library and Information Science Conference.

Darch, C., C.-M. Karelse, P. Underwood, 1996. "Alternative routes on the super-highway". *The Sunday Independent,* 5 May: 9. Available on-line at http://164.88.55.4/online/hero.

Department of Education, 1996. *National Commission On Higher Education. Report: Framework for Transformation.* Government Printers: Pretoria.

—, 1996. *Technology Enhanced Learning Investigation in South Africa: A discussion document.* Government Printers: Pretoria.

Ford, B. J., 1995. "Information literacy as a barrier." *IFLA Journal,* 21: 99–101.

Hall, R.; W. Rex and C. Sutherland, 1995. "Overcoming barriers to learning: A draft report on research conducted by the E.O.R.P. into non-classroom-related factors affecting academic performance" Equal Opportunity Research Project: UCT. Available: http://www.gu.edu.au/gwis/ins/infolit/blueprnt.htm

Kanter, J. 1995. "Computer-information literacy for senior management". *The Executive's Journal* 1 (3).

Karelse, C.-M. and P. Underwood, 1996. "Seeking answers on the super-highway". *The Sunday Independent,* May 12: 6. Available on-line at http://164.88.55.4/online/hero.

—, 1996. "Advancing information literacy education in South Africa". *Academic Development,* 2 (2), Academic Development Unit, UWC.

Kuh, G. D. and L. L. Baird, 1992. "A landmark in scholarly synthesis". *The Review of Higher Education.* Spring, 15 (3).

Kuhlthau, C. C., 1993. "Implementing a process approach to information skills: A study identifying indicators of success in library media programs". *School Library Media Quarterly,* Fall.

Laurillard, D., 1993. *Rethinking University Teaching: A framework for the effective use of educational technology.* Routledge: London.

Lennox, M. F. and M. L. Walker, 1993. "Information literacy in the education process". *The Educational Forum,* 57 (Spring): 312–324.

Liebowitz, B., 1995. "Transition: Acquiring academic learning at the University of the Western Cape". *Academic Development,* 1 (1).

Makhubela, L. and Z. Koen, 1995. "Another angle on access: information literacy and student learning". *Academic Development,* 1 (1).

Marais, J. J., 1994. "Information literacy and quality of life". *Free State Libraries,* July/September: 13–19.

McClure, C. R., 1994. "Network literacy: A role for libraries". *Information Technology and Libraries,* June: 115–125.

Nahl-Jakobovitz, D. and J. Jakobovits, 1994. "Bibliographic Instructional design for information literacy: Integrating affective and cognitive objectives". *Research Strategies,* 11 (2).

National Education Policy Investigation, 1993. *Adult Education.* Cape Town: OUP/NECC.

Nichols, J., 1993. "Library orientation: A workable alternative re-worked". *Library Review,* 42 (7).

Olanlukun, S. O. and N. A. Kuye, 1994. "Academics and the power of information: The comparable effects of information group term papers among college students". *South African Journal of Library Science,* 4 (2): 159–162.

Rader, H. B., 1994. "Library orientation and instruction – 1992". *Reference Services Review,* 22 (2): 79–95.

—, 1995. "Information literacy and the undergraduate curriculum". *Library Trends,* 44 (2), Fall: 270–278.

Reinhart, A., 1995. "New Ways". *Byte,* March: 50–62.

Ruth-York, D., 1994. "Students in the library: Paper for research into higher education conference". York University, United Kingdom, December.

Sayed, Y. and K. de Jager, 1997. "Towards an investigation of information literacy in South African students". *South African Journal of Library Science.* 65 (1), 5–12.

South African Government, Dept. of Education, 1996. Green Paper on Higher Education Transformation, Pretoria.

—,—, 1997. Technology Enhanced Learning in South Africa: A Discussion Document; Report of the Ministerial Committee for Development Work on the role of technology that will support and enhance learning, Pretoria.

—,—, 1997. A Programme for Higher Education Transformation: Draft Education White Paper 3, Pretoria.

South African Parliament, 1997 Higher Education Bill 75A-B, Government Printers, Cape Town.

—, 1997, Higher Education Act 101/1997; Pretoria, Government Printer.

University of the Western Cape, 1994. "Lifelong, continuing education for the 21st century: A submission to the National Commission on Higher Education". Cape Town, University of the Western Cape.